SHADES OF GREEN

SHADES OF GREEN

Myth and Muddle in the Countryside

David Sinclair

GRAFTON BOOKS

A Division of the Collins Publishing Group

LONDON GLASGOW
TORONTO SYDNEY AUCKLAND

Grafton Books
A Division of the Collins Publishing Group
8 Grafton Street, London W1X 3LA

Published by Grafton Books 1990

British Library Cataloguing in Publication Data
Sinclair, David
Shades of green: myth and muddle in the countryside.
1. Great Britain. Rural regions
I. Title
941'.009'734

ISBN 0-246-13258-2

Phototypeset by Computape (Pickering) Ltd, North Yorkshire
Printed in Great Britain by
William Collins Sons & Co. Ltd, Glasgow

CONTENTS

1	The Country Habit	1
2	Field and Wood	27
3	First in a Village	59
4	The Call of Nature	87
5	Problems of Development	115
6	O'er Vales and Hills	145
7	A Country Living	175
	Further Reading	193
	Photo Credits	194
	Index	195

ONE

The Country Habit

The country habit has me by the heart,
For he's bewitched for ever who has seen,
Not with his eyes but with his vision, Spring
Flow down the woods and stipple leaves with sun

Victoria Sackville-West, 'The Land'

The countryside has rarely been out of the news in Britain during the 1980s. Reading the newspapers, watching television, listening to the radio, entering a bookshop, one could have been forgiven for thinking that ours was a small peasant economy intimately concerned with and dependent upon the minutest shift in agricultural practice or rural balance. Sometimes it has seemed almost as if Sir Robert Peel were still Prime Minister and the condition of the countryside remained as important as it was in the days of the Anti-Corn Law League, so extensive have been the debates, so fierce the passions aroused.

One faction has cried constantly that the countryside is in mortal danger from greedy developers whose only motive is profit; another has kept on roaring that farmers are killing every wild thing in sight and threatening the very soil on which we stand through over-use of machinery and chemicals; still another has been continually heard ululating over a decline in bird population, or the loss of hedgerows, or the disappearance of marshland, or the appearance of coniferous forest. There has been a proliferation of action groups dedicated to stopping the construction of roads, airports, railway lines, factories, shopping centres and houses in rural areas, while multifarious organizations have become accustomed to expending their time and energies in monitoring and reporting on the state of grassland, water, trees, moorlands, uplands, lowlands, birds' eggs, wildflowers, badgers, historical sites and countless other aspects of the landscape and its inhabitants. Newspaper articles have expatiated at length on the merits of organic farming or the future of the National Parks, while reporting almost daily some pronouncement on rural topics from one or other concerned body. Television documentaries, beautifully photographed and heart-rendingly elegiac, have lingered lovingly over 'threatened' bucolic beauty, and the 'nature programme' – on radio, too – has become as much a part of the standard output as the soap opera, the situation comedy or the quiz show.

At a less altruistic level, the countryside most recently began to be perceived as an asset in terms of personal fulfilment and, incidentally, personal investment, prompting jaded urban workers and retirees to scour the land for rural real estate in a seemingly desperate search for 'a better life', so that even redundant agricultural buildings never intended for habitation were commanding six-figure selling prices if they possessed the combination of charm, age and view considered the ideal qualities of the contemporary 'country home'. (The word 'house' is never used in this connection today, for to British ears, attuned to the softest of social nuances, it means something altogether different; country homes, not country houses, are what most people buy in these supposedly more egalitarian times.) After years of decline, brought about by economic restructuring, the rural population began actually to increase, notwithstanding the fact that, economically speaking, the countryside has become even more peripheral in the post-industrial age than was the case during the rapid and necessary urbanization of the smokestack era.

Such a degree of interest and activity has placed the countryside closer to the top of the political agenda than it has been for decades. To be sure, agriculture was politicized a long time ago, and the political element has become infinitely more noticeable in the highly charged atmosphere of the European Community, but the rise of a new class of ruralists with firm ideas and loud voices has meant that there are votes in them thar hills. It is a myopic politician who does not see the potential of the conservationists, countrified commuters, protectors of wildlife and pursuers of a national natural heritage who regularly rear their heads from every one of the last remaining hedgerows and cast long shadows over what are left of the leafy lanes. Indeed, the Conservative Party, sensing a risk of losing its monopoly as the modern guardian of the rural interest, has found it necessary to refurbish its countryside credentials in the face of rebellion in the shires. Market forces and private enterprise have to take account of a new form of parish-pump politics which cares more for the village green than for the provision of more houses or better services. Even Margaret Thatcher, reaching the end of her first decade as Prime Minister, has attempted to shed her image as the 'Iron Lady' of the Falklands conflict and trade union reform in favour of that of a 'Green Goddess', embracing current environmental concerns. Meanwhile, the great government offices of Foreign Secretary and Home Secretary have found themselves in danger of being upstaged by that of Secretary of State for the Environment: only an obsessive concern for law and order and the minutiae of broadcasting have allowed the Home Office to compete for attention with the Environment Department, while the Foreign Office has laboured away largely unnoticed.

It might be thought – indeed, it is widely assumed – that it must be good for the countryside to be returned to the central position it enjoyed in British life long ago. After all, the British Isles have a rich and varied rural landscape of which their inhabitants can be justifiably proud, and such an asset is surely worth protecting from careless exploitation that might ultimately lead to its disappearance. Yet there are several worrying aspects about the new rural mania that suggest it might finally do the countryside more harm than good. The 'country habit' to which Victoria Sackville-West alluded in her sentimental poem 'The Land' shows every sign, in its modern manifestation, of being just that – an instinctive and often thoughtless reaction that has nothing to do with the real value of the countryside or the deeper currents of rural life. In the blinkered, narrow-minded and often selfish desire to 'save', the question of what role ruralism and the countryside should play in contemporary society has never even been asked, let alone answered.

One of the least beneficial assumptions of the current clamour is the identification of the countryside in general and the landscape in particular with the past, the insistence on the part of those who claim to have the best interests of ruralism at heart that their aim is to protect what they glibly refer to as 'our heritage'. This wildly over-used term is seriously misleading, not least because nobody appears ever to have asked what it means.

The assumption is that the landscape is our living link with our history, the visible expression of our British roots, and that if we allow it to change ('to be destroyed', the conservationists would say), the link is broken forever. This view is palpably nonsensical. Our national identity is not defined by the background against which we carry on our lives: if that were true, we might find large parts of the British Isles claimed as their 'heritage' by the mainland descendants of Celts, Romans, Angles, Saxons, Jutes, Danes and Normans, all of whom helped to create the landscape that is now regarded as quintessentially 'British'. There is, in fact, no single thread that can be identified as our rural heritage or tradition, but rather a bewildering array of different influences that have combined haphazardly through the centuries as successive invaders and immigrants and, later, successive generations, have reconstructed the landscape according to their own needs and ideas. What the conservationists seek to preserve is simply the landscape *as it is now*, in its incarnation of the late twentieth century. Far from affirming history, this approach actually denies it, for it would remove the continuous change without which history does not exist: if the present becomes the same as the past, there is no point in distinguishing between the two.

Where, for example, does the 'traditional' landscape begin and end? If we take the period when the British Isles were born, nearly 8000 years ago, when rising sea levels separated them from mainland Europe, we discover that the conifers so hated by conservationists today were one of the most important features of the scenery, along with birch and willow: the 'English' oak and the much-loved elm were later immigrants from the warmer south. As for fauna, our 'traditional' species included reindeer, rhinoceros, bison, hippopotamus and elephant – but where are they now?

Perhaps we should do better in the search for our heritage to consider what the countryside looked like when man first appeared in what we think of as Britain. That would take us back 35,000 years, to the emergence of our ancestor *Homo sapiens sapiens*, who found himself in an Arctic landscape of ice and tundra. The remnants of that traditional scene can be found only in the highest mountains of Scotland, while the rest of Britain has changed beyond recognition, and in any case at that distant period, the British Isles simply did not exist.

Obviously, then, we must move further forward in time if we are to discover identifiable traditional elements in the landscape we now see about us. Yet if we do that, further difficulties emerge. The retreat of the last glaciation (known as the Devensian period) almost 11,000 years ago was accompanied by a relatively rapid warming of the climate, which gradually converted the open, Arctic tundra into dense forest. This presented a serious challenge to Stone Age man, who began to find that the grazing animals upon which he depended for food were disappearing as their habitat retreated before the encroaching trees. From that point on, allowing for complex fluctuations in the present overall climatic phase (the Flandrian), and the severance of Britain from the mainland, the chief influence on the landscape of these islands was not natural but human.

In order to survive, the nomadic Stone Age inhabitants were forced to turn increasingly from hunting to farming, with the dramatic effects on flora and fauna that remain familiar to us today. By the Neolithic period, between six thousand and four thousand years ago, substantial stretches of woodland had been cleared – creating, in the opinion of some experts, the chalky downlands of southern Britain, for example – and others had been coppiced. The burning of forest and subsequent ploughing had begun to create areas of bog and blanket peat where drainage had been restricted. Human interference in the fragile ecology of the uplands led to the destruction of their woods, producing open heath and moorland upon which trees are only now reappearing, again through the efforts of man (and often in the face of fierce opposition from 'traditionalists' who ignore the fact that such areas were once forested). As the quality of prehistoric tools improved, some stretches of forest were felled to provide grazing for domesticated animals, while grasses and cereals were deliberately encouraged because of their usefulness to man. Even the shape of the country-side was changed as mining began to cut into hillsides, and in some places soil deterioration set in as the growing population demanded perhaps the earliest form of intensive farming.

The technological advances of the Bronze Age accelerated land-scape changes. It was during this period – three thousand to five thousand years ago – that large-scale forest clearances took place in areas such as the Lake District, the Pennines, the North York Moors, Dartmoor and parts of Wales, an ambitious agricultural endeavour that has ironically resulted in those districts being pro-tected today. The succeeding Iron Age, during which the climate was considerably wetter and colder than it had been, saw a retreat from many upland areas, but the depredations of agriculture had so altered the soils that they were unable to return to their former wooded glory. Today these man-made derelict sites form the bulk of our National Parks and 'areas of outstanding *natural* beauty'.

If our wildest and most valued landscapes are the result of human handiwork, it is clear that in seeking 'traditional' scenery we must base our judgements on factors that are cultural rather than purely natural. Indeed, since what we see is most often not what we think we see, we might do better to forget about nature altogether. Many geographers and academic environmentalists agree that the varying scenic beauties considered among Britain's glories are almost entirely the results of human intervention, and that much virgin landscape was destroyed in the process of creating what has survived. Since we are part of the natural order, there is nothing intrinsically wrong in regarding the signs our ancestors have left as our landscape heritage, even if they conflict with what untamed nature intended. Where we tend to run into difficulty, however, is in failing to allow for the imposition of one tradition upon another, earlier one, and in refusing to recognize the effects and therefore the importance of the element of continuity in the impact of humans on their environment.

The Romans who invaded Britain in AD 43 were, in their time, efficient despoilers of the rural landscape through their construc-tion of great roads and dominating military installations. The Fosse

Way, running from Exeter to Lincoln, must have had much the same scenic effect as the M25 does today, while Hadrian's Wall and its forts were considerably more intrusive upon an 'unspoilt' northern landscape than is the present Fylingdales early warning station. Time has lent enchantment, however, and these constructions, which would certainly have been the subjects of bitter public inquiries now, have acquired the patina of historical glamour. On the other hand, the remains of Roman Britain we jealously guard represent a mere fraction of what the invaders did to the environment; the rest was carelessly swept away in the face of other cultural, economic and social – and equally alien – imperatives. If it had not been so, many of the features of the British landscape so prized in modern times would never have existed.

According to popular myth, it was the next wave of invasion that established the foundations of the British, or more specifically the English, countryside as we know it. The marauders of the fifth century who became the settlers of the sixth – Angles, Saxons and Jutes, known collectively to the native British Celts simply as Saxons, though all identifying themselves as Angles (hence England) – are credited with imposing upon the land a pattern of rural settlement and organization which formed the basis for everything that came after it. In fact, the more we learn about the history of the countryside, the less tenable such assumptions become. Contemporary research suggests that the development of village life was a much more gradual process and that the idea of the Saxons creating a rural tradition which has existed to this day is simply not true. Many of the rural features widely supposed to date from time immemorial are, it is beginning to be realized, of much later origin. Certainly the idea of the 'traditional' village green as the nucleus round which Saxon villages were built has been shown to be false: even in many of the lowland regions most intensively settled by the Saxons, greens are uncommon and where they do exist are often of a much later date. Some came about by accident, where holdings were no longer occupied; others developed as market-places and still others were actually designed long after Saxon times to give to new villages the impression of what was believed to be a historical quality.

Conversely, many settlements fondly ascribed to the Saxons on the grounds of plan or name are actually much older. The settlers simply took over Roman estates or expanded Celtic villages and gave them new names, so that the traditions now associated with them are far from clear-cut. Neither was the Saxons' effect on the pattern of agriculture as dramatic as has long been thought, though certainly their superior ploughs enabled heavier land to be cultivated than had previously been the case. Again, detailed investigation has shown that the famous open-field system attributed to the Saxons was not some sort of farming revolution but rather a gradual change founded upon methods that had been in use for centuries. It was only towards the end of the Saxon period, in the ninth century, that open fields began to have a marked effect on the landscape. The reasons for this remain improperly understood, though they were probably to do with the pressures of an increased population which required more land to work and greater amounts of food.

The next great tradition of rural development that is probably less reliable than it appears is the Norman Domesday Book, painstakingly compiled in 1086 on the orders of King William I for a purpose that remains somewhat obscure. Many villages proudly claim mention in 'The Book of Judgement', but others known to have existed at the time of the survey are omitted, as is a great number of cities and large towns, notably London and Winchester, together with the whole of Wales and the northern counties of Northumberland, Cumberland, Westmorland and Durham. Domesday, then, was by no means a geographical record – its aims appear to have been fiscal, military and legal – and while it presents a fascinating portrait of medieval society, the landscape which it divides into taxable units can for the most part only be guessed at. For example, the fact that a manor with a specific amount of land is located in a particular place does not necessarily indicate that a village was nearby, while alternatively the assessed extent of a particular lord's holdings might encompass a number of settlements not mentioned by name. Moreover, a variety of methods was used in classifying land tenure and extent (possibly reflecting local usages in what was, after all, far from a unified cultural entity), so that the impressions gained can be confusing.

We may guess with some accuracy at what the population of England was towards the end of the eleventh century, based on the figures given in the Domesday Book and other, local sources, but so far as the actual appearance of the landscape is concerned, much lies in the realm of imagination. It is clear that by far the greater part of the virgin forest that had covered these islands had been destroyed by the time of the survey and that the agrarian scene now so dear to English hearts had begun to take shape. Yet there were vast tracts of wasteland, not untouched by human hand but destroyed and depopulated by that only too human activity, war: these it would be the task of the later generations to restore, leaving their own impression that had nothing to do with Domesday. The authors of the thoughtful *Penguin Guide to the Landscape of England and Wales*, Paul Coones and John Patten, highlight the fallacies of a modern vision of rural Britain based on the Domesday model:

The conception of the English village as a solid, unchanging and, by implication, more or less thoroughly understood element of the traditional scene is almost embarrassingly inadequate. Some villages moved, shrank or wasted away; others continued in various ways the intricate process of development which had begun in Saxon times or even before, perhaps incorporating planned elements, or expanding into towns or being engulfed by them. The vast majority of medieval villages were not created at a particular time and preserved unchanged in the visible landscape; rather the Middle Ages contributed to a continuous process of settlement change still going on today. The identification and assessment of this contribution are made even more difficult because we know so little about the appearance of medieval villages. Only the more elaborate buildings, constructed of stone, such as churches, manor houses and the occasional barn, have survived. The peasant hovels of mud, timber and thatch had to be rebuilt at short intervals because they decayed and collapsed.

Indeed, the process of change to which Coones and Patten refer was itself marked throughout the Middle Ages as a result of famine, plague, war and economic decline. Nobody was on hand to wave preservation orders, and as climatic or social conditions altered, so did the landscape. There was also a certain amount of what some zealous conservationists call agricultural vandalism as hedgerows were ripped out, to make holdings more viable in the light of improving technology and 'modern' methods, while at the same time a wave of new enclosures took place as landlords sought to protect their incomes and their power: the idea, popular in some quarters now, that we are all inheritors of the land simply by virtue of being born on it is difficult to sustain. It is worth pointing out, too, that thousands of acres were left uncultivated for the sole purpose of hunting and killing their wildlife, a 'traditional' land-scape element that would not find much favour among the environmentalists of today. (Though some animals and birds were protected by royal decree, the purpose of their conservation was to provide a plentiful supply for the nobility to eat, a practical connection that has no place in modern ecological thought.)

It was during the period between the end of the Middle Ages and the beginning of the Industrial Revolution that many of the most significant features of the present British landscape came into being. I say significant because they were almost entirely the result of human effort, because the changes were on a scale and of an effect comparable only with the clearances of virgin forest in prehistoric times, and because they represent dramatically the role of man in the development of the environment.

Already towards the end of the medieval period, the idea of farming as a subsistence occupation was beginning to wane and greater efforts were being directed towards growing crops for sale. The expansion of economic activity during the sixteenth and seventeenth centuries confirmed agriculture as very much a business – indeed the chief engine of trade – and its position as such was further reinforced by the new wave of enclosures brought about by Acts of Parliament from the seventeenth century onwards. The visible effects of the enclosures were marked, not only in terms of new boundaries that erased traces of 'traditional' arrangements but also because of new roads that displaced twisting peasant tracks as the primary means of communication. These practical alterations coincided with fundamental changes in attitude: for the first time human beings began to see themselves as both the most important element and the supreme power in the terrestrial scheme of things, capable of creating order out of what appeared to be natural chaos. As western society moved towards what is called the Enlightenment, the conviction grew that nature must not only be exploited but also tamed and rearranged according to a human vision. It was the beginning of what might be termed the designer-countryside.

The desired effect of the so-called 'Improvers' was a gentle, lush, regular landscape, with decorative trees and murmuring waters to give the impression of peace and contentment – the sort of scene described by the eighteenth-century writer Oliver Goldsmith:

> How often have I loitered o'er the green,
> Where humble happiness endeared each scene!
> How often have I paused on every charm,
> The sheltered cot, the cultivated farm,
> The never-failing brook, the busy mill,
> The decent church that topped the neighbouring hill,
> The hawthorn bush, with seats beneath the shade,
> For talking age and whispering lovers made.

The sight of unharnessed nature, by contrast, was at that time considered horrible; visiting the Scottish Highlands in 1753, Goldsmith was disgusted by what he called a dismal landscape and hideous wilderness, while one of his contemporaries called the Highlands 'part of the creation left undressed; rubbish thrown aside when the magnificent fabric of the world was created'. Another poet, Thomas Gray, on a visit to the Alps in 1739, wrote of 'the permission mountains have of being frightful'.

The point, for those seeking a landscape tradition in the golden age of English ruralism, is that such a tradition is in all its essential features anti-nature and pro-change, which is the precise opposite of the modern ecological ethic. There is a fond belief nowadays that our ancestors of the seventeenth and, perhaps more particularly, eighteenth centuries were more in tune with their environment than we are: if they were, it is simply because they lacked the technology to improve soil artificially or to compensate for the vagaries of climate and crop disease. Where they could intervene in the interests of greater efficiency, they did so, draining wetlands, creating watermeadows, felling trees, cultivating open heath, introducing new crops. In fact, some of their activities were extremely unsound in ecological terms, such as the famous case of the Bedford Level in East Anglia, where in the mid-seventeenth century a large-scale draining scheme (which incidentally caused severe disruption to traditional grazing, fishing and peat-cutting) resulted in river blockage with flooding elsewhere and serious subsidence as the drained peat dried out. Elsewhere, whole villages and even small towns were razed and often rebuilt in other locations as the all-powerful aristocratic landowners redesigned the landscape according to their tastes, even to the extent of including carefully constructed, suitably picturesque 'ruins'.

Another point to be made is that what has survived from those Elysian days is not necessarily what it appears to be. To quote again from Coones and Patten:

> The grand designs and substantial houses of the rich have lasted comparatively well, but it is difficult to see examples of the transient houses of the poor. Almost all the older buildings represent the homes of the better-off; even country cottages which are all the rage these days are rarely true cottages – however tiny they seem to modern eyes – but small farmhouses, and many are not, in their present form at least, very old. The prettified aspect presented by so many 'period houses' today is as far removed from the realities of any past period as are the tastes and occupations of their present occupants or weekenders.

Nor was the rural scene entirely as beautiful, tranquil and uplifting for the soul as Goldsmith and others seemed to find it. Coones and Patten note:

It is likely that the poor man's dwelling changed little over the centuries. They were neither built to last nor constructed by craftsmen. The antiquary, William Stukeley, visiting the bleak marchland of Cumbria in 1725, found the houses of the cottagers 'mean beyond imagination, made of mud, and thatched with turf, without windows, only one storey; the people almost naked'. Conditions such as these were commonplace in a society where severe poverty was endemic. For thousands the so-called 'flowering of rural England' simply seemed to pass them by and signalled little change, while the 'age of the improver' actually marked a decline for those whose livelihood was ruined by the enclosure of the commons and the reclamation of the wastes for the benefit of the rich or up-and-coming.

From the late eighteenth century onwards, the progress of the Industrial Revolution signalled the end of Britain as a nation of countrymen, and perhaps helped to implant in folk memory the comforting myth of a lost world in which mankind lived in closer harmony with nature, or the fond dream of somehow returning to find one's roots in ruralism. The greater the spread of the terrace and the factory, the office and the suburb, the more the realities of the countryside receded, until a life governed by unremitting labour and the vagaries of the weather was transformed in clouded perception into an idyll of health and happiness. The new urban masses, having left the farms and fields in droves to seek security, a better standard of living and greater opportunities in mill and foundry, found that as industrialization took hold and expanded, all these things were, in general, provided. Conditions in the industrial towns were far from ideal – indeed, they were frequently appalling to modern eyes – yet they nevertheless represented material advance, which had the effect of keeping the newcomers in the towns and attracting even more migrants. At the same time, however, the obvious disadvantages of the new urban life, not least its overcrowded nature, prompted continual backward glances through the smoke and grime towards the meadow and stream, where life was supposed to be free and clean.

These nostalgic visions were too fleeting to notice that most farmworkers and their families lived in unrelieved wretchedness, poor, in bad health and – in spite of the abundance surrounding them as new techniques increased yields – badly fed. Between 1873 and 1900, for example, industrial wages increased on average by about 16 per cent, with at the end of the period skilled workers in London and most other large cities earning thirty-six shillings a week or more. An agricultural worker, by contrast, received just fourteen or fifteen shillings a week in 1900, a rise of one shilling on what he had earned in 1874, or precisely half that enjoyed by even unskilled workers in the cities. As one observer in the mid-nineteenth century noted, farmworkers could not be said to live, merely not to die. Yet still rural life was commonly seen as something to be envied, and 'escaping' into the countryside whenever possible became a growing fashion. Partly this was because even many of those grown rich from industry and commerce had bucolic dreams too: the new mercantile élite often sought to announce their arrival on the social scale by emulating the old aristocracy and building country houses.

Of course, I have oversimplified. The effects of industrialization and rapid urbanization were considerably more complex than I can indicate here: a good number of town-dwellers looked down upon their country cousins, showing contempt for their lack of sophistication, supposed ignorance and narrow horizons. Most of the well-to-do who acquired country estates were careful to keep one foot firmly in the city, recognizing its advantages, while the majority of ordinary people knew in their hearts that they were better off in an urban existence whatever its disadvantages. So it was that the countryside, in the minds of many, became closely associated with leisure, the scene of a sort of half-life that was only vaguely related to everyday reality. Consequently, ruralism lost its central position in the economic structure, the concept of it as an organism with its own dynamics began to recede: to the growing numbers of people not living in it, what the countryside looked like became more important than what it actually did.

This change of view has intensified in the twentieth century, for several reasons. Between 1900 and 1950, the built-up area of

Britain doubled, so that the landscape changed drastically. It was not simply that there were more houses and industrial or commercial sites, but also that the vastly expanded urban population required more services to sustain it. Roads and reservoirs had to be built, electricity pylons erected and, perhaps even more important, agriculture had to provide more food from less land, which meant greater mechanization, larger fields, wider use of artificial fertilizers and pesticides, and more activity in marginal areas (which are often those now considered to be the most beautiful). At the same time, as urban life was accepted as the norm for a growing population and the motor car really began to make its presence felt, cities and towns became less and less comfortable places in which to live, the need for the countryside as an escape became more pressing and the yearning for the mythical and idealized rural existence of old grew even stronger.

The effect of all this, combined with an increasing awareness of and interest in ecology and 'the environment', was to create a perception of crisis in the countryside, but a crisis that for most of those who sensed it had less to do with actual rural life than merely with the landscape. The conviction grew, mostly among urbanites and those well enough placed to be able to choose to live in the country and continue to work in the towns or to retire to some rural haven, that while change (almost always for the worse) was running out of control in urban areas, the countryside must be protected from change, preserved as they dreamily imagined it had been for centuries, or even returned to that imaginary state if it had already been 'desecrated'.

Ironically, this desire to prevent change has led to changes perhaps more significant than any the countryside has experienced in its long history. Their significance lies in the fact that the popular concept of rural life has now become utterly unrelated to reality, unconnected with the fundamental socio-economic base that for centuries kept the countryside functioning. Living in the country has acquired an entirely new meaning, one that has nothing to do with living in the fullest sense of the word. Those who hanker after what they think of as traditional have apparently forgotten the greatest rural tradition of all – a countryside that works. In their manic desire to save, the well-meaning conservationists may be poised to destroy, for a countryside without a reason for its existence will surely cease to exist, becoming indistinguishable in all but superficial appearance from the urban background of most of those who in the late 1980s have been stampeding to claim their little bit of heritage. When the fad comes to an end, what will be left? A protected landscape in itself will not provide sufficient justification for anyone to wish to live in the houses left by those departing in search of the next dream. In the drive to retain our version of rural tradition, what contribution will we be making to it? If all we do is preserve what has been left to us, there will be no tradition of our own for our descendants to build on.

From the brief outline I have given it is obvious that the single most tangible – 'traditional', if you like – link between the Neolithic forest-clearers and the agribusiness of today is in the capacities to change and to adapt to change. Of course, change is not always for the better, but even when it appears to be for the worse it is better than stagnation, for it will surely itself be followed by more change. Modern theories of physics, and even of medicine, are leading to the conclusion that apparently random change – chaos, the scientists call it – is an essential ingredient of life. Research has shown that when the rhythms of energy and matter become too orderly and stable, it is often in preparation for death. That is something on which those who labour and lobby to preserve things in their present form would do well to reflect. Nor can the argument be sustained that the modern age is out of step with natural rhythms and is therefore bound to destroy them. A glance at the history of the planet will show that this has always been true, that the human species is itself one of the more powerful of those rhythms (though its dominance is not as assured as it likes to pretend). We change our surroundings because we ourselves are changing, and the fact that this is inevitably an unsettling and unpredictable process is the reason for our collective tendency to look backward even as we are moving forward. The past always seems more comfortable because it is finite. The mistake of the rural protectionists, and others, is to imagine that the past remains appropriate to the present, even that it remains at all in any vital sense. As the weekly newspaper *The Economist* pointed out in 1988:

> Like many British political ideas, the notions of citizenship and community are based on a sentimental view of what rural life was like. People caring about each other's welfare, families holding together, villages and small towns with their own schools, their own cottage hospitals, the bobby on his bike ... Real Britain is mostly quite different. Its cities are a kaleidoscope of races, attitudes and behaviour. One third of all marriages end in divorce, so more and more 'families' involve single parents or step-parents. Young Scots leave their small towns to work on London's building sites and sleep in barges and caravans. Even homeowners, now two thirds of all households, move on average twice every seven years. As for the villages, they are increasingly peopled by weekenders with Volvos ...

The gap, succinctly expressed in those few telling sentences, between the real and the imaginary is another disturbing factor of the new ruralism, and implies social consequences that could be far-reaching. The vision has become more important than the fact, the wish more to be pursued than the need. Many of us now, it seems, would rather use resources to save crumbling old barns and decayed stone walls than on building reasonably priced housing for country people who are being forced to move to the towns because they cannot compete financially with the well-heeled urbanites who see the countryside as nothing more than a pleasant place in which to sleep and spend their leisure hours. We allow schools, shops and post offices in villages to close, thereby destroying much of their vitality, yet we mouth pious homilies on the continuity of rural life and the importance of preserving the village atmosphere and appearance. We complain about the damage and disruption caused by an increased amount of traffic, but we most often claim it as a victory when fields are left undisturbed by new roads that would relieve congestion. From the windows of our rural retreats we would rather watch people trudging off to town to collect their unemployment benefit than have a small, well designed, non-polluting modern factory impinge upon a corner of the view.

There is, moreover, a punitive, authoritarian and even somewhat vicious side to this self-important posturing on behalf of the environment (which, as well as being taken to mean only things that are green, is also frequently referred to as 'disappearing', suggesting that future generations will live surrounded by nothing). Apart from the anti-blood sports and 'animal rights' terrorists spawned by rampant and sometimes childishly misguided nature-love, and the urban guerrillas of the 'free access to the countryside for all' movement, institutionalized forms of rural repression have emerged. The picking of wildflowers may now be a criminal offence, which would have amazed and infuriated the inhabitants of the rural past so admired today. In 1987, the Marquis of Hertford was fined £10,000 with £5000 costs after allowing a field which he owns, but which happens to cover the remains of a Roman settlement, to be ploughed to a depth of ten inches. No sign of the first-century settlement is visible; to all intents and purposes the field in question has the appearance of a field, but the fact that it is there and decreed by law to remain just as it is for ever allowed the English Heritage organization to prosecute his lordship. It makes no difference, apparently, that we cannot see what the Romans left behind, or that ploughing the field in no way detracts from our knowledge that there was once a settlement there. The soil itself has become hallowed ground.

'The message of this case,' a representative of English Heritage said grimly, 'is that we are determined to press prosecutions when legally protected sites are damaged and to extend this protection to those which do not have it. The casual damage to important archaeological sites has gone on too long.' It has, of course, been going on for two thousand years or more, and if it had not most of the present population of these islands would be homeless.

Perhaps the saddest part of the attitude of English Heritage and so many of its conservation colleagues lies in its materialism, the sense that the past cannot exist unless it can be seen or touched or, at the very least, labelled. History is no longer permitted to be part of the spirit or imagination – it must be experienced with the senses, in material form. It is as if we cannot be sure the Romans were here unless we can walk where they walked, see what they saw, or understand the feudal system unless its agricultural boundaries are there in front of us. We have shaken off so many of the habits of the past, and are grateful for that, yet we seem unable to reconcile that progress with the casting aside of the detritus of history in order to further or even simply to keep pace with our advance. We convert and modernize old houses with our electricity, natural gas, sanitation systems, central heating, fitted kitchens and double-glazing, so that the buildings in fact bear little relation to what they were when they were built, yet we shrink from replacing them with new, more efficient, more appropriate structures because we cannot trust the past unless our contact with it is physical.

Now we apply this same materialistic sense to our landscape and wildlife, preferring to cling to decline and decay rather than to enjoy the past of the mind and build new life upon its physical manifestations, even though we have at our disposal unprecedented means of recording both past and present and even of reconstructing history in its physical form if we wish to. The landscape as it is now could be preserved forever in vision and sound and, with advanced bio-technology, recreated on a small scale, so that future generations could see precisely what it was like while at the same time benefiting from the developments we should have freed ourselves to bring to it. Preservation on the vast scale on which we practise it is not only unnecessary, it is also anti-social. Nobody really wishes life to be lived as it was by our distant ancestors, and to confine ourselves as a matter of policy to the landscapes they knew is an affront to social progress.

This leads to other anti-social elements in the new ruralism as an institution. The creation of National Parks, Areas of Outstanding Natural Beauty (most of which, as I have indicated, are natural only in the sense that the men who created them are part of nature) and all the other definitions of the conservation ethic has led to a multiplicity of laws, rules and regulations that impinge upon virtually every aspect of rural life in the regions where they are applied. As the 'no-change' brigade gains in respectability and influence, the degrees of compulsion and infringement of individual liberty threaten to increase. Already in many substantial areas of the countryside, people are unable to do as they wish with land or property they own; recently it has been seriously suggested that there should be limits on where they may buy property. National Park fanatics have expressed support for the promulgation of new laws preventing the purchase of holiday homes in what are called 'sensitive areas', which means districts where landscape considerations make the planning rules so strict that building new houses is all but impossible, so that an artificial shortage of property is created to the detriment of everyone who lives or wants to live there. The idea that people should only settle where they do not interfere with the scenery is surely a sinister one.

It was perhaps not surprising, therefore, that in 1988 the suggestion that the muddled English concept of the National Park should be extended to Scotland was received there with suspicion and alarm. Though Scotland contains many of the other scenic structures of institutionalized conservationism, it was spared the development blight of National Park designation when the Parks were arbitrarily created in 1949, mainly because the Scottish proponents of the idea were sensible enough, unlike their English counterparts, to see that the scheme would only work if any land so designated was nationalized. In the event Scotland's escape did not greatly benefit its development (though it may have made it easier for the North Sea oil industry to flourish), but to impose National Park restrictions now on its depressed rural economy would be to add insult to the injury of its history of endemic disregard by increasingly southward-looking British governments. It would be even more insulting at a time when the value of the English and Welsh National Parks is being ever more seriously questioned, even in their own conservationist terms. The newly resurgent Scottish National Party expressed its total opposition to the idea, no doubt sensing that National Park designation is a convenient method by which government can dispose of difficult areas. Turn them into National Parks and they can safely be left to their official protectors and the tourists: there is no need to formulate development policies for them because no real development is possible. It was a fate to

22

which the 8000 or so small farmers who grub a meagre living out of the Scottish Highlands were understandably reluctant to see themselves condemned.

By contrast there are richer and, to the urban taste, more hospitable parts of Britain which it is clearly not the intention of government to forget. These fall almost entirely in the lowlands and most especially in the south-eastern counties easily reached from London, which makes them ideal resting places for the new breed of converted or part-time countryfolk. Unfortunately, those same rolling acres are also a magnet to industry and commerce, which is growing tired of the congestion, inconvenience and high costs of London but is reluctant to move too far away from what – through a mixture of selfishness, short-sightedness and sheer inertia – has been allowed to become the sole significant decision-making centre in the land. Hence the dilemma of Mrs Thatcher's administration. On the one hand, the Conservatives borrowed from the philosophy of the thirtieth President of the United States, Calvin Coolidge, and declared that the business of Britain was business. On the other hand they found themselves forced to trim their expansionist sails when faced with the dangerous currents of a new ruralist movement determined to maintain every still un-developed corner of the Home Counties in a state as near as possible to that in which they imagined the Saxons (or at least the Victorians) had left it. The Department of the Environment, in consequence, donned the mask of Janus and set about trying to relax the mortal grip of the planning laws while at the same time presenting the face of the committed conservationist to the pro-liferating 'environmental' interests for whom development means restoring the old and keeping the new at bay for as long as possible.

One can sympathize with the Department's difficulties. By any objective standard, the ramified mass of planning restrictions affecting rural areas, particularly where the complications of legally supported landscape definition have been superimposed, have seriously hampered the prospects of reviving a national rural economy that has been in decline since the Industrial Revolution and will, unless something can be done, suffer grievously from the agricultural cutbacks that have begun to be imposed as a result of

23

gross overproduction of food in the United States and Western Europe. Farming is already losing its potential as an employer, and little enough has.been done – partly owing to the planning system – to provide alternative employment for country-dwellers in the places where they live. That problem can only grow more acute as further contraction of agriculture takes place. Along with it comes the question of what is to be done with the thousands of acres of farmland that will be taken out of production as the inevitable retrenchment proceeds.

Yet it is easy to see, also, that the conservationist case is not without merit. Visions of a countryside covered in subtopian building are unnecessarily alarmist; but it would clearly be unwise to unleash market forces on a landscape that is not only attractive but that also offers potential and resources which cannot be measured simply in terms of commercial balance-sheets. The careless destruction of plant and animal life, or the removal of a spirit-uplifting view, for no reason other than that they are inconvenient, are neither morally justifiable nor practically sensible, since each living thing has its part to play in the evolutionary process of which mankind is only the pacemaker. The relative value of human against other forms of life is a deeply philosophical matter, and perhaps we swing too easily from one extreme to the other – the current debate about using animals for medical experiments is not something our ancestors would have spent much time discussing – but it does not require a great deal of thought to appreciate that existence would be dull indeed if its more utilitarian aspects were to be all that motivated us. Scenery is worth saving, and just for its own sake. The point is, though, that the unquantifiable benefits of a pleasant environment are enjoyed most by people whose practical needs have been satisfied, so that conservation only becomes entirely appropriate where its social costs have been fully examined. To deny many people jobs, houses and amenities merely so that a few of the more privileged may gaze dreamily over the meadows is, in my opinion, morally reprehensible and socially divisive.

What we as a nation must do is to consider and implement a coherent policy that makes the best of our rural resources, in whatever form they take, for the benefit of the overwhelming majority of our people. That means conservation must be justified equally with development and in each case *all* the needs of the specific area in question must be objectively assessed. Erecting 'Keep Off' signs on thousands of acres in which people live and work is no more sensible than building on every available plot. Nor should the language of confrontation and crisis be permitted to distort decision-making, as it is now. Landscape, whether legally protected or not, is going to change anyway, and the matter of how it will change – insofar as that is under human control – is the only point at issue. Obviously a building is going to intrude upon a view, but equally obviously our senses are conditioned to appreciate architectural as well as natural beauty, otherwise we would not wish to save old cottages or barns that are 'traditional' parts of the landscape. It is a question of reconciling the two, and not talking in terms of 'loss' or 'destruction' but rather of gain and improvement. Moreover, buildings have appeared and disappeared throughout history. Today's factory might well be tomorrow's picturesque ruin or might even disappear, like Lord Hertford's Roman settlement, under a blanket of grass.

Protected landscapes, as we are beginning to discover, also change, very often as a direct result of the effort to save them. The effects of encouraging tourism in such areas and of regulating patterns of settlement through strict planning controls can contribute to serious landscape erosion, economic stagnation and social disintegration, leading to decay. Properly managed and designed development – taking account of all the environmental considerations, not just those affecting the landscape – can help to ensure conservation and maintain or improve economic and social balance.

As to rural life itself, that is a more complex matter, one on which we cannot legislate (though the present level of activity suggests that, in our arrogance, we are determined to try). One thing is certain, though; if the countryside continues to be seen as primarily an escape from the perceived discomforts of the town, a policy that integrates the needs of country and town, from farmer to factory worker, will be impossible to achieve and both rural and urban life will suffer as a result. This book is an attempt to synthesize the various aspects of the rural end of the equation. It examines and questions some of the basic assumptions, often misplaced and sometimes absolutely contradictory, that have led to the present confusion about the countryside, from agriculture to tourism and the pressures for both development and conservation. The impression has been carefully fostered by special-interest groups that there is a general crisis in the countryside. There is not, partly because there is much more of it than the doomsayers like to pretend. What there is, however, is a series of challenges which must be faced coolly, without the waves of hysteria that now break so regularly over various aspects of British life and can lead to changes that are ill-thought-out and frequently counterproductive.

Most books written about the countryside rely heavily on emotional appeal, either perpetuating the great rural myth or presenting what are considered the most beautiful regions of Britain as being in mortal danger. As someone long familiar with country life, I have tried to avoid sentimentality and nostalgia on the one hand and hysteria on the other. Keeping the idyllic qualities of my childhood in remotest Northumberland exactly where they should be, in memory, I have attempted to look beyond the propaganda and examine the facts, to identify what precisely *is* happening in the countryside, what effects present and future changes might have and whether we should be concerned about them, and finally to suggest ways in which we may develop our attitudes towards rural matters in order to develop the countryside in a manner that is sensible in visual, practical, economic, environmental and, above all, in human terms.

Professor Howard Newby, a leading sociologist who has written several books on rural matters, has commented that the countryside is too important for its future to be decided by default. I agree, but I would add that it is also too important to be handed over to conservation zealots, commuters, weekenders and tourists. We must rid ourselves of the bad old 'country habit' and construct a new vision of country life founded on reality. If we do not, our descendants may never forgive us.

26
—

TWO

Field and Wood

Now some folks say
There ain't no hell
But they don't farm
So they can't tell.

American farmers' protest song

It is a truism, though it often seems to be forgotten, that the central feature of rural life is farming. Even today, when almost 80 per cent of the population of Britain lives in cities and towns, nearly 80 per cent of the land area of the country is still devoted to agriculture of one sort or another. The future of the countryside, then, depends very much upon what happens to farming, and the future of agriculture depends entirely upon what society decides it wants from the people who provide the basic requirements for its survival. The problem is that a nation composed overwhelmingly of urbanites can see only dimly how the countryside works, and even then its vision is distorted by sentimentality on the one hand and prejudice on the other. Consequently agriculture, like so many other aspects of ruralism, is beset by a bewildering clash of perceptions and a fair amount of both ignorance and hypocrisy – in addition to which farming, since the Second World War, has fallen increasingly under the heavy hand of government, with politicians determining what should be produced and how much it should cost. The result of all this has been to drive agriculture into a crisis that has, as we shall see, profound implications for the countryside as a whole.

There are throughout Britain about 217,000 farms covering approximately 40 million acres, the largest proportion of agricultural surface area of any European country with the exception of Ireland. Those farms produce nearly 80 per cent of all the temperate food the country needs and Britain, once a net importer of foodstuffs, is now in the position of being a net exporter. Between 1977 and 1987, according to the Ministry of Agriculture, the volume of agricultural production in Britain rose by more than 20 per cent, despite falls of 2 per cent in the area farmed and 10 per cent in the work-force. 'Yields of all major crops have risen by about 2 per cent a year, with wheat reaching 3½ per cent,' the Ministry reported. 'This has had a dramatic effect. For instance, the proportion of home grown wheat in the British loaf has increased by 50 per cent and, instead of being a net importer of cereals, we are now the sixth largest exporter in the world.' Looking back over a longer period, milk output has doubled since the war, the wheat harvest has increased by five times, the barley yield is six times greater, and the production of poultry meat has risen eightfold.

On the face of it, this is a remarkable success, with many farmers proudly claiming it as the greatest achievement in any sector of the British economy since 1945. 'Successive British governments have provided the farming industry with a basic framework of support which recognizes its special nature,' boasted the Ministry of Agriculture in 1987. 'Britain's initial postwar agricultural policies sought to build on the successes generated by the urgent wartime and postwar need to produce as much food as possible at home. Farmers responded to the incentives to greater production and used the advances in technology. As production expanded, the emphasis shifted towards efficient production ...' Further incentives appeared in 1973, when Britain became a member of the European Community, chief among whose activities was the support of farming through the Common Agricultural Policy, or CAP, designed to increase agricultural productivity; to ensure a fair standard of living for farmers; to stabilize markets and maintain the availability of supplies; and finally to ensure that such supplies could be bought by consumers at reasonable prices.

One of the main features of the CAP is its price guarantee system, which covers 94 per cent of agricultural produce in Europe and operates in four main ways:

1. Permanent or conditional guarantees of crop price or sale, which means in essence that when market prices fall below a

certain level, the Community intervenes to buy up stocks at guaranteed prices for storage and eventual sale.
2. Protection for European farmers against competition from lower-priced products from outside the Community.
3. Direct subsidies paid to farmers depending on the types of crops planted – for instance, hard wheat, olive oil, oil seeds and tobacco.
4. Flat-rate subsidies based on the area planted or the amounts produced of certain crops.

It was this system – together with a multiplicity of national and Community grants to enable farmers to modernize, mechanize, make a profit from poor land and so on – that provided the incentive for European agriculture to achieve unprecedented levels of productivity and efficiency. As one British farmer put it, 'Between 1970 and 1980, our cereal yield doubled: that would normally have taken a century.' By the mid-1980s, however, it was becoming clear that the Common Agricultural Policy suffered from serious structural defects. To put it another way, most of the assumptions that had spawned it were wrong.

It had certainly achieved its first aim of increasing agricultural productivity, but only at the expense of vast surpluses, leading to the wholesale destruction of some perishable crops and the costly stockpiling of others. As the British Ministry of Agriculture admitted not long ago, the rate of advance in food production since the war outstripped all forecasts. At the same time, the total amount of food consumed in Britain changed hardly at all. Much the same was true of the rest of Europe, which found itself with more farm produce than it knew what to do with. At the end of 1987, for example, Community food stores contained more than a million tons of butter, three million tons of barley, five million tons of wheat and hundreds of thousands of tons of beef, milk powder, veal, pigmeat, sugar, sheepmeat and other products.

There had also been a significant rise in the living standards of farmers across Europe, but that perhaps had less to do with the CAP than with a reduction of two-thirds between 1958 and 1988 in the number of people earning their living from the land. And

31

while the market for agricultural products had been stabilized in Europe, there were serious distortions in the world market as a result of the dumping of surpluses by the Community at knock-down prices. Then there were the enormous costs of the CAP – which for the system of guaranteed prices alone rose from 3928 million European Currency Units (Ecus or 'green pounds') in 1973 to 19,744 million Ecus in 1985. Not only did these make it impossible for the Community to finance other aspects of its policies, but they actually threatened to bankrupt the whole undertaking. Meanwhile, though the generous pricing system helped farmers considerably, it ensured that consumers in the Community, as well as paying heavily through taxes to finance the CAP, were obliged to spend more on food than necessary, since the guaranteed prices paid to farmers were almost always higher than those on the open world market, sometimes four times higher.

A further significant disadvantage of the CAP was that its bureaucratic and complex system of grants, subsidies and export refunds proved not only to be expensive but also to provide rich pickings for unscrupulous producers. An official report published in 1988 estimated that the level of fraud in the EC agricultural sector was running at some $60 million a year. Since that figure was based on only a limited number of random checks, it seems likely that a systematic investigation would yield evidence of abuses that cost European taxpayers many millions more.

Growing political and public disquiet about the mistaken assumptions of the CAP led, in 1984, to the beginning of an agricultural crisis from which the industry as yet shows no sign of recovering. Farm ministers of the Community agreed that agricultural spending should in future rise more slowly than the EC budget as a whole, but external factors such as a sharp fall in the dollar actually increased CAP spending during 1984–6: in Britain, for example, it rose from £1368 million in 1984 to £1840 million the following year. At the same time, the surpluses encouraged by open-ended price guarantees continued to increase. Thus it was that in 1986 the Community politicians took the decision that, after forty years of continuous and desired expansion, agricultural production must go into decline.

The imposition in 1986 of limits on production and penalties for farmers who over-produced sent tremors of alarm and outrage through the industry, but that was only the beginning. Governments soon discovered that a policy formulated during the food shortages of the last war and immediately afterwards, having continued virtually unquestioned for forty years, had also become institutionalized to the extent that, now questions were being asked, it had become almost impossible to change without either destroying the entire structure of agriculture created by it or by pouring even more money into a system already proved to be too expensive.

As recently as February 1988 *The Economist* noted that the British Ministry of Agriculture, which the paper described as 'the farmers' poodle', was continuing, in the face of both surpluses of millions of tons of food and frantic efforts to cut production, to give 'its one declining industry £1½ billion a year in price support; plus £150 million for special areas, mostly for hill livestock; and £100 million in capital grants'. The situation behind those figures is a ridiculous one. Not only is government paying farmers to produce too much and then in effect paying again to buy the surplus from them, but it is also handing out grants and subsidies in order to stop them producing while maintaining their incomes.

Yet there is more than one way of looking at the relationship between the state and the farmer. On closer examination, it is not at all clear which is the poodle. Essentially, the official assumptions about agriculture have turned farmers more or less into government employees dependent upon the state for their incomes. As the Ministry of Agriculture has pointed out, 'Sudden cuts of a size sufficient to bring supply and demand into balance would devastate farm incomes and hence the rural economy.' Neither, since they are not employed in the same way as, say, steelworkers were when the industry was still nationalized, can farmers easily be given their cards and told their services are no longer required. They, in a sense, are the pets that the government cannot simply abandon: that brutal expedient was tried in 1920, when the comparatively modest subsidies introduced to prevent mass starvation during the First World War were abruptly withdrawn, leading to widespread

33

bankruptcies among farmers, mass unemployment in rural communities and dereliction in large areas of the countryside, so that by
1939 national starvation was again a real possibility. In the present
crisis, therefore, everyone is a victim – the farmer, the government
and the taxpayer who has to foot the bill.

Farmers feel not only threatened but also betrayed and resentful:
once national heroes, they have come to be seen by many people as
greedy villains soaking up subsidies that protect them from unpalatable economic realities. The attitude of *The Economist* is one
that is widely shared, as witness this comment from *The Sunday
Times*: 'The farm lobby, like the navy, regards its subsidies as a
national asset, a patriotic levy on every man, woman and child to
preserve a corner of the English way of life, no questions asked.'
Even the Prime Minister, Mrs Thatcher, has felt it necessary to
chastise the National Farmers Union, telling it in a letter that 'You
are ready to acknowledge the problems of over-production. But you
seem unwilling to face up to the consequences of tackling them.'

The farmers argue that they have simply been doing what was
asked of them and that they have now become victims of both their
own efficiency and a sudden change of political emphasis, 'from
landed interest to suburban salariat,' as the writer Simon Jenkins
expressed it. For the best part of half a century, farmers say, they
have been encouraged to increase their yields, to make each acre
more productive and keep food cheap and plentiful by more
intensive methods, such as greater use of machinery, artificial
fertilizers, weedkillers and insecticides. Now they are told that they
are, in effect, too efficient and must become less so, which seems to
mean that while the government boasts of increased standards of
living for the British people, those of farmers must inevitably
decline.

There is undoubtedly some merit in their case. Like so many
other industries that have suffered cruel and unusual punishments
in a changed political climate, agriculture was over the years lulled
into a false sense of security under the corporatist consensus of
postwar British society. Now that consensus has broken down and
a fashion for market forces and entrepreneurship is in the
ascendant: suddenly Samuel Smiles, the nineteenth-century

prophet of self-help, has been resurrected as an idol of the late twentieth century. Standing on one's own feet and earning one's own living are the new catchphrases. The creeping nationalization of British agriculture, however, has meant that farmers have been kept away from the real marketplace for so long, many of them do not know where it is any more. Similarly, government has taken upon itself so much responsibility for agriculture that it finds it difficult in both practical and political terms to discover an acceptable way out of the corporatist net.

These are not the only problems for agriculture. Along with the perception that intensive farming produces more than anybody wants there has arisen a sense that the food produced is of poorer quality than that grown 'organically' and that it might even be harmful because of the amount of chemicals used to maximize yields and kill pests and diseases that would otherwise claim part of the crop. In the case of livestock, there is a strong strand of liberal opinion which holds that factory-farming methods are a barbarous and cruel affront to what are becoming known as 'animal rights', and again that the use of artificial means to promote growth and obtain the greatest amount of saleable meat might be dangerous. Moreover, the rapid mechanization of farming, and the greater – some say indiscriminate – use of chemicals, are increasingly viewed as being ecologically and environmentally unsound. Hedgerows and copses are grubbed up to make bigger fields that are easily managed by ever larger machines: in consequence, wildlife habitats are destroyed and the landscape is reduced to featureless prairie. Fertilizers damage soil, causing chemical breakdown that requires the use of more fertilizers in order to keep the land productive; they also pollute water supplies. Pesticides and herbicides kill insects and plants upon which animals and birds feed, causing perhaps irreversible damage to the ecological balance. The widespread use of silage rather than hay robs the countryside of meadows and therefore wild flowers, some of which now exist mainly on the uncut margins of motorways. Much of this, according to rapidly expanding and increasingly vocal lobby groups, known variously as conservationist, environmentalist or 'green', is the fault of farmers, who as countryfolk should know better.

The environmental pressure-group Friends of the Earth says that the cost of our second agricultural revolution is being paid in soil erosion, polluted water and chemically polluted foods. The Council for the Protection of Rural England, while giving credit to farmers for performing so well in economic terms, complains that in turning the countryside over to technology we have sacrificed what it calls 'the natural bits' – woodlands, wetlands, hedgerows, wildflowers and so on. Some environmentalists argue that farming must cease altogether in those parts of the country they classify as most damaged by over-use of chemicals, specifically nitrates. Eastern England has been particularly badly affected, they say, citing high levels of nitrates and pesticides in drinking water. Many farmers cry 'Rubbish' to the claim that they are destroying the landscape and damaging the countryside, arguing, for example, that they now have more woodland on their holdings than would have been found in previous years. But for the present it is the conservationists who have captured public perceptions, to the extent that in 1989 an official of the Ministry of Agriculture stated that it was now government policy 'to keep the landscape as the public wants it to look'.

The coincidence of the realization that we are producing and paying for more food than we can handle and the awakening of 'green' concerns has caused a most interesting situation. The government's desire to, in the words of the Ministry of Agriculture, 'cut back by encouraging farmers to turn to commodities not in surplus, to use land less intensively than now or to take it out of agricultural use', has combined with the campaign of the environmentalists against intensive farming to bring us almost to the point where we are ready to make a giant leap backwards along the road of progress. Environmentalists are quite clear about it: they want the agricultural revolution to 'go into reverse'. Like King Canute, we seem to be poised at the water's edge to try to turn by order the tide of history – forgetting that Canute's purpose in the old story was to demonstrate in dramatic form what a vain, stupid and pointless exercise it was.

The prevailing wisdom seems to be that we must ignore the agricultural developments of the past half-century, either by pretending that they never happened, which is what the green lobby would like, or by paying farmers not to take advantage of them, which is the solution of the government. The Prince of Wales, whose views on environmental matters have made him the darling of the liberally-minded middle classes in the forefront of the conservation movement, let it be known in 1988 that he had decided to revert to what are generally referred to as 'traditional' farming methods on the 770 acres of his Gloucestershire estate, Highgrove. 'It is just a return to the ways used fifty years ago, which owed more to husbandry than to chemicals,' said the prince's farming manager. That is just the sort of thing calculated to appeal to the romantic view of the countryside that has gained such currency during the past few years. As one real farmer put it to me, 'You know what they really want? They want us out in the fields with smocks and scythes. It makes pretty pictures, you see.'

The fact is that the ways of fifty years ago required long hours of often back-breaking toil for farmworkers. The fact is that traditional methods of husbandry reduce crop yields, on average, by at least 20 per cent, and therefore income. The Prince of Wales might be able to afford the loss, but few working farmers today could. The fact is that switching from conventional to organic farming generally means a gap of up to five years before a worthwhile crop is obtained: how is a farmer to earn his living in the meantime? The fact is that organically-grown foods cost about 40 per cent more than those produced by intensive farming. The Ministry of Agriculture says rather smugly that there is a premium for foods such as free range eggs, beef and lamb produced under extensive husbandry systems ('extensive' meaning the opposite of intensive in farming terms), but it cannot deny that organic foods are a small part of the market and that 'most people will continue to want wholesome food at the lowest possible prices'. It is true that retailers have done well out of promoting organically-grown produce and are ready to buy more of it, but with about 13 per cent of the population dependent on social security benefits and some 50 per cent still earning less than the average wage of £245 a week, the number of people willing and able to pay premiums for their food is limited at present and is likely to remain so for some time.

Even among conservationists, the more enlightened admit that the scope for organic produce is extremely small.

What the politicians and the environmental campaigners seem incapable of understanding is that their perceptions of the country-side in general and farming in particular involve not abstract theory or a vision of some ideal world, but the lives of real people (not only farmers, either) and one of the foundations of the social and economic structure. The food industry as a whole in Britain – from farming to processing and manufacturing, retailing and catering – is worth some £40 billion a year, employs about 2 million people and contributes something like 5 per cent of the country's gross domestic product. Changes in the structure of the population (rising numbers of elderly people, of married couples who both work, of single people) mean that the most significant growth area in the industry is in prepared foods, a situation very different from that of fifty years ago. If the industry is moving forward in line with changing tastes and demands, experimenting with new preser-vation techniques and novel ways to maintain flavour without the use of artificial additives, where is the sense in insisting that its basic source of supply, agriculture, reverts to out-of-date practices? The chief merit in such a course appears to be that it would satisfy the nostalgic longings of the conservation lobby, the spreading but entirely erroneous belief that once upon a time the world was somehow better than it is now, and that reversing the trend of development is the simplest way of dealing with what is, admittedly, a very difficult problem.

There are other solutions, but they lie in the future, not in the past. Along with most other industries, farming and food pro-duction has invested heavily in research to provide a new and wider range of crops, to keep prices down, to reduce the levels of fat in meat, for instance, in the interests of a healthier diet, and to find alternative uses for surplus food products. Although the Agri-cultural and Food Research Council is in the midst of a reduction of £11 million in the financing it receives from the Ministry of Agriculture, it is doing its best to raise more money from the industry and from interested charitable sources in order to exploit what the council calls great scientific opportunities. 'Biological research', says the Council, 'has now reached the stage where the application of modern techniques, especially at the cellular and molecular levels, is opening up new ways of understanding how plants, animals and microbes work and how their performance might be controlled much more precisely than in the past.'

Among projects financed by the council that show significant promise are genetic engineering techniques that will allow the creation of new strains of disease-resistant potatoes; the development of non-toxic methods to combat cereal viruses which currently cause losses of up to £100 million a year in Britain; the production of a new strain of Cox-type apple, called Fiesta, with the texture, flavour and keeping qualities that might help British growers to regain some of the market share lost to the heavily promoted French Golden Delicious. One of the most important areas of research, however, is the formulation of new crops for arable land that will have to be taken out of production to reduce surpluses and new uses for the surplus crops themselves. The introduction of oil-seed rape has been a great success (though environmentalists have objected to it on aesthetic grounds) and tests are being conducted to see whether sunflowers, which produce better quality oil, can be introduced to more northerly regions. There is also considerable potential for the growing of linseed to produce oil for industrial use and for flax as a fibre crop, which could create a whole new processing industry. Protein-rich lupins, of which we import about 100,000 metric tons annually, offer another opportunity. There are exciting prospects, too – and not only for agriculture – in the alternative use of existing crops. Denmark and Sweden have taken the lead in experimenting with cereals as sources of chemicals for paper-making, plastics, pharmaceuticals and even energy. Again this could produce a complete new industry, with a network of factories separating and treating the harvest. The British potato crop could be increased by half a million metric tons if there was investment in plant to produce potato starch for the paper, paint and plastics industries, which currently depend heavily on imports, while a new technique invented in Britain by ICI could lead to the production of a revolutionary biodegradable plastic made from fermented sugar.

The picture of agriculture as a 'declining industry' casually drawn by *The Economist*, then, is not necessarily an entirely accurate one. It is, however, a reflection of what has become the fashionable (and, it must be said, essentially urban) view – even, it sometimes seems, a wish. That it is peddled at all is an example of ignorance, prejudice, suspicion, wrong-headed attitudes and sheer lack of thought.

So far as the so-called environmentalists are concerned, their reverence for the past and apparent distaste for the present blinds them to the possibilities for the future. Many claim sententiously that their aim is to preserve the countryside for the benefit of the generations to come, yet their attitudes are conditioned by current assumptions and make no allowances for the inevitable changes that will distinguish those generations from our own.

Another point worth bearing in mind is that if the scientists are right and the earth's climate is warming as a result of the 'greenhouse effect' (the emission of large amounts of carbon dioxide into the atmosphere from the burning of fossil fuels), we shall need all the agricultural technology at our disposal to meet the challenges of drought, flood and widespread famine that may arise as the predicted climatic changes of the next fifty years affect the growth patterns and yields of food crops. The droughts, heatwaves and warm, dry winters of the late 1980s wreaked havoc in the grain-growing areas of the United States, the Soviet Union, Canada, China and South America, raising the price of wheat by 50 per cent and, in 1989, reducing the world's supply of staple foods to enough for only 61 days. The effects were felt most seriously, of course, in poorer countries such as Ethiopia, Bangladesh, Sudan and Vietnam, but even in rich America there were growing fears of food shortages, which the administration began to regard as a more dangerous threat to international stability than the spread of nuclear weapons. Scientists were divided over whether the apparent changes in climate – a rise of 0.5 degrees Centigrade in mean world temperatures over just five years – represented a natural phenomenon or were the result of the greenhouse effect, but, whatever the cause, they offered a warning to those who talk of reversing the agricultural revolution. It is the future to which we must look, not the past.

As for official attitudes in Britain, we find yet another example, as if one were needed, of politicians thinking ahead no further than the next election and dealing with a difficulty in terms of what will produce the most rapid and obvious short-term gain, by means that are simple and familiar. Regrettably, most farmers have become so dependent on Whitehall that their reactions are equally predictable and merely add to the conspiracy that prevents the development of a sensible policy for the development of rural areas and of agriculture in particular.

That changes are necessary in agricultural structure and practice is unarguable. To quote *The Economist* again, 'even the EEC cannot hurl money at its surpluses for ever,' while the environmentalists actually do have a point when they relate intensive farming to senseless destruction, even if their response to it owes more to sentiment than practicality. Thus far, however, nobody has emerged with the vision and imagination to weave all the strands together and create an approach that would result in the emergence of the agricultural industry we shall need in the future, together with sensible measures to protect the environment from needless abuse and a structure that would make economic sense.

As recently as 1978, according to the government's Countryside Review Committee, which produced a series of reports in that year, the main thrust of farming policy was to expand food production in the United Kingdom, with the objective of increasing the net product of the agricultural industry by 2½ per cent a year. Within that objective 'most benefit was likely to come from higher output of milk (with its by-product beef from the dairy herd), sugar beet, cereals and sheep meat'. The intervening decade has seen a complete turnabout, with the Ministry of Agriculture noting in 1987: 'Already the establishment and tightening of quotas has begun to curtail over-production in the dairy industry. Changes in the beef support system will make an impact on surpluses there. A programme including land diversion, alternative crops and other appropriate measures is needed if we are to tackle the cereal mountains and the other surpluses effectively.' Small wonder that farmers, who had for example increased dairy herds and devoted more acreage to cereals, were outraged when quotas and pro-

41

duction levies were introduced. As the Ministry itself pointed out, 'quotas can freeze the structure of the industry, preventing low cost producers from replacing high cost producers and making it difficult for new entrants to come into the business. As time goes on, the farming industry may lose out ...'

The government's response was what had become the traditional one throughout the European Community: subsidy and grant. This time, though, instead of paying farmers to produce more, public money was devoted to encouraging them to do less, to do something quite different, or in some cases to do nothing at all. During the financial year ending in March 1987, for instance, the quaintly named Milk Outgoers Scheme designed to reduce dairy-ing produced a bill of £9½ million. The fall in the total number of dairy cows was marginal and milk production actually rose by 1 per cent. As that financial year ended, the 'new' approach to agri-culture, agreed by European Community members, was codified in the British parliament through an announcement that £25 million was to be made available to farmers willing to diversify – that is, to engage in non-farming enterprises – and to 'extensify', which means to make their land less productive. In other words, while agriculture continued to be subsidized to the tune of some £1½ billion for what it did produce, it was also to receive a huge amount of money to persuade it not to produce.

At the heart of this enterprise was the 'set-aside' scheme, under which £16 million was made available in 1989, £22 million in 1990, to farmers prepared to allow 20 per cent of their best land to lie fallow for five years. The National Farmers Union, accustomed to complaining about government 'cuts' and quotas, gave this idea a cautious welcome, even suggesting that instead of the voluntary system envisaged by the Ministry of Agriculture, set-aside should be made compulsory, no doubt because it would help farmers to stay in business and maintain their incomes regardless of forced reductions in their output. The union was much less enthusiastic about an alternative extensification scheme suggested by the Council for the Protection of Rural England, which, predictably looking over its shoulder, proposed that farmers should curtail the use of chemical fertilizers, reduce the level of grazing, revert to the age-old custom of field rotation and leave some of their land for the benefit of flora and fauna. This might well benefit the countryside in the terms in which it is viewed by the Council, but the consequent reduction in output would be of little help to farmers for whom greater crop yields have come to mean larger incomes/ subsidies.

The conservationists could claim a victory, though, with another aspect of the government's new strategy, which was to designate what are known as Environmentally Sensitive Areas, or ESAs, and to pay farmers (naturally) to work them with due consideration for the landscape and ecology. In return for an annual payment of £100 a hectare (just under 2½ acres), a farmer agrees not to plough or reseed grassland, so as not to destroy a diverse 'plant community'; not to use more than a small amount of chemical fertilizer; not to use herbicides except for some limited spot treatments; not to drain land where wetland species flourish; to maintain traditional walls, hedges and barns; and to seek advice on the management of any farm woodland. In some places, farmers undertake to restrict liming of land and spreading manure and to cut hay (in order to preserve meadows) instead of the more efficient silage.

'In these selected areas,' said the then Minister of Agriculture, Michael Jopling, 'we shall be offering farmers incentive payments to continue the more traditional farming methods and maintain the beauty and wildlife value of their farms.' Or, as a weary Yorkshire farmer commented to me: 'The reason they want us to cut down on muckspreading is so the countryside smells better for the trippers.'

It is indeed difficult to avoid the impression that we have strayed into some sort of agricultural fairyland, with farmers being paid to supervise unused fields, to use outmoded methods and to act as official wildlife wardens. Nor is there much economic or practical sense in the way we seem to have chosen to go about adjusting farming to changed conditions, or for that matter protecting the environment. On the one hand, the government is prepared to spend £12 million a year on nineteen Environmentally Sensitive Areas, where the landscape and ecology are thought to be worth preserving and protecting, yet on the other hand it is spending more than £20 million a year in capital grants and £111 million on livestock compensatory allowances to keep farms going in what are called the Less Favoured Areas of Britain. These cover the country's wildest and most beautiful landscape and actually include ESAs such as Loch Lomond and Breadalbane in Scotland, two areas in the Cambrian Mountains of Wales, various parts of the Pennine Dales and the region of Mourne at the south-east tip of Northern Ireland. In effect, then, we are paying one farmer to make the best of his holding in a marginal area and paying another in the same area not to make the best of his holding, at least in business terms.

The conclusion may be unpalatable, but it is surely obvious. We could protect the environment, substantially reduce public spending on agriculture and contribute to a decline in surplus food production by discouraging farming in marginal areas rather than continuing to encourage it or, what is worse, encouraging it as we are doing by paying farmers to run their businesses at what amounts in normal commercial thinking at a loss. In this connection it is worth noting that the condition of British industry is frequently said to be better than it has been for years, with productivity and profits rising, notwithstanding the halving of government subsidies between 1979 and 1987. Farming, meanwhile, which is considered to be in crisis and declining as an industry, has seen its subsidies rise over the same period from £830 million to £2.2 billion.

The government, the environmentalist organizations and the agricultural industry itself have done no good by co-operating, albeit often unwillingly, in reducing farmers to what is essentially and increasingly playing at farming. Sooner or later the truth will have to be faced: there are in Britain too many farmers producing too much food on too much land. The National Farmers Union admits that some five million acres of agricultural land will have to go out of production by the end of the century, though it is naturally wary of committing itself to serious ways of achieving that reduction. Other estimates suggest that the overcapacity is more like ten million acres, while still others reckon that in the long term 85 per cent of the land currently used for farming will prove surplus to requirements. Put this together with the fact that 53 per cent of the agricultural area of Britain – more than 20 million acres containing about a quarter of the country's farmers – is considered difficult to farm and merits special subsidies, and some idea of the way forward may begin to emerge. It never did make sense, except to those with some nightmare vision of mass starvation, to pay farmers to continue doing what they did on land that was not really suitable for the purpose. There is no justification, except in fantasy, for claiming one is preserving a way of life which has existed for centuries when the injection of large amounts of public money alters that way of life almost beyond recognition.

Moreover, even with the vast amounts of public money thrown at it, agriculture is not the moneyspinner some people imagine. Figures from the Ministry of Agriculture itself show that in real terms farm incomes in 1986 were no higher than they had been in 1980: subsidies may help to increase production, but they apparently do not add to the farmer's standard of living. Based on an index of 100 for the year 1980, the figures show that farm business income per holding, which had reached a peak of 135 in 1984, was back down to 102 by 1986, while total farming income in the same year had an index of only 97. In 1988, the incomes of the 140,000 largest farms dropped by 25 per cent. In the meantime, the level of borrowing by farmers, though still relatively low in industrial terms, has been rising steadily. On average, farms in Wales showed 12 per cent of their assets as external liabilities; for English holdings the figure was 15 per cent and in Scotland as high as 21 per cent. It has been estimated that the total of loans outstanding against British farmers is not far short of £6 billion. With incomes likely to fall further, some of those borrowers will undoubtedly go into bankruptcy or be forced to sell their holdings. Many others will only just stay in business. In that sense at least, farming is a declining industry, and the sort of policies that have been adopted merely serve to prolong the agony. In this respect, recent reports by the Samaritans organization suggest a perceptible rise in the number of farm suicides or threats of suicide. In 1986, one of Britain's best-known farmers, the broadcaster Ted Moult, killed himself because of worries about the way his business was going. The present atmosphere of uncertainty helps no one, least of all the farmers.

To be fair, the government has understood that many farmers are going to have to stop farming, at least in the conventional sense, hence its diversification and rural enterprise schemes. A number of farmers, too, have decided to bow to the inevitable. Some have turned to what might be thought of as fringe areas of agriculture, such as rearing goats, or angoras for the increasingly popular cashmere trade; breeding snails for the catering industry; growing mistletoe for the Christmas market, or crops such as borage which are in demand for pharmaceuticals. The farmhouse bed-and-breakfast trade is well established, but now there is a trend towards full-scale hotel accommodation, even offering conference facilities, or survival training, which has become popular as a method of further education and personality development for business executives. At least one farm has become a centre for the growing numbers of people who seem to want to spend weekends playing war-games. For the most part, however, diversification means nothing more than running another business alongside farming, which might raise the farmer's income but is very far from the restructuring the industry really needs.

Unfortunately, the most positive step the government has tried to take to reorganize agriculture appears to be the least popular. Part of the £25 million diversification programme announced in 1987 was a new Farm Woodland Scheme intended to supplement the existing grant system which encourages afforestation. Britain and the rest of the European Community, while awash with food products, are seriously undersupplied with home-grown timber. British forestry supplies only about 15 per cent of the country's needs and, according to the Ministry of Agriculture, the proportion is unlikely to rise beyond a quarter by the end of the century. In Europe as a whole, half the amount of timber required is imported. This is partly a result of the misdirected drive to produce more food. Many acres of woodland in Britain were cleared in order to release land for crops: figures are difficult to obtain and often unreliable, but the Countryside Review Committee found in the late 1970s that during the previous twenty-five years, as much as 80 per cent of the trees had been lost in arable areas of the eastern counties, where the average size of farm fields had doubled.

The decline of forests in a country once covered by them began to cause concern as long ago as 1919, when the Forestry Commission was set up by the government first to manage the woodland belonging to the Crown Estates and then to engage in a national strategy for tree-planting and forest management. The Commission ultimately became the largest single landowner in Britain, but its activities alone were not sufficient to enhance the country's timber resources, and it was not until after the Second World War, with the situation becoming critical, that any serious effort was made by governments to involve private landowners in tree-planting on a large and commercial scale. Even then, as we have seen, it remained more attractive financially to devote land to growing food: the returns were not only quicker, they were also more or less guaranteed. Also, the nationalizing Labour Government of 1945 was more interested in state-owned forestry and set the Commission an eventual target of 5 million acres (of which, by 1988, it had achieved getting on for two-thirds).

Successive governments attempted to implement some sort of national forestry policy, but it was not until 1979 that a comprehensive review was undertaken, resulting a year later in the forestry grant scheme for landowners and, in 1985, further grants for the planting of broadleaved woodland, together with an attractive tax regime reflecting the long-term investment required by forestry. These arrangements resulted in the creation of nearly 200,000 acres of new private commercial woodland in five years. In 1987, Britain had about 5 million acres of productive forest, more than half of it in private hands. This, of course, was still woefully inadequate and, taken in conjunction with agricultural surpluses, seemed to present an excellent opportunity to redirect the efforts of farmers.

There have been two problems, however. The first was that farmers felt the woodland grant of £50 an acre for twenty years, in the case of conifers, or thirty years for broadleaves was too low. Then there was the conservation lobby. The self-styled protectors of the countryside had long criticized the Forestry Commission for the creation of large forests that had what they considered to be an undesirable 'visual impact' on the landscape, and even more for its bias towards faster-growing conifers. In her emotive and pejorative book *This Land is Our Land*, the militant environmentalist Marion Shoard summed up the attitude of many of her kind towards coniferous trees:

> In place of the rounded, bushy-topped trees that have for so long complemented the rounded curves and gentle hills of Britain march more and more ranks of regular, spiky-topped conifers. They strike a chill into lowland landscapes, stripping them of the seasonal variety provided not only by the ever-changing colour and shape of foliage of deciduous trees but also by the galaxy of flowers and bushes that thrive in Britain's traditional deciduous woodlands but not among conifers. In place of the bosky delights recorded in our woods by our poets, there is increasingly to be found a gloomy emptiness.

Various arguments are deployed in the campaign against conifers: they support only sixteen different species of insect, as against the more than 280 that may find sustenance in deciduous woods; the number of animal species that prey on insects is thus considerably reduced; there are many fewer herbaceous plants, ivies, mosses and lichens in coniferous woodland; their impact on the ecosystem, according to Shoard, 'is almost as devastating as if the land had been cleared to make way for a barley field or a motorway'. Worse still, it seems, is that conifers make financial sense, and God forbid that the countryside should be exploited for profit, even though the 'traditional' and 'natural' beauty so prized by the environmentalists is almost entirely the result of just such exploitation, stretching back thousands of years.

Conifers mature in twenty to thirty years, whereas broadleaves need between sixty years and a century before they can be usefully harvested. Furthermore, hardwoods are much less used than softwoods – as one forester put it, broadleaves are for looks, conifers for production. Unfortunately, however, the partisan formula that conifer equals destruction has been widely taken up, so that it is now hallowed as an unchallengeable assumption. No doubt I shall be violently rebuked for saying that in my opinion conifers often actually improve the landscape, as in the bare mountains of West Wales where I used to live and where Forestry Commission plantations have added grandeur to a vista that would otherwise be bleak and forbidding, covered by the scars of long defunct lead mines. A wide variety of plants thrives along the forest roads, wide paths and clearings and along the banks of the many streams that traverse the forests to feed the network of lakes in the district. That my pleasure in such a landscape is not unique may be seen from the number of visitors who take advantage of the Commission's policy of public access. Yet the anti-conifer attitude appears to prevail, and when private forestry companies began seriously to take advantage of the government's planting incentives, the outcry reached a climax.

There seems in many cases to be a connection between concern for the environment and somewhat vague political views of what might be termed the 'soft left' variety, which deplore the profit motive, mistrust businessmen in general, and landowners and farmers in particular, and regard what others call progress as being invariably inimical to the life of the planet. Private forestry has become a special target for people holding such opinions, not only because to them it represents the despoliation of the countryside but also because they see it as wicked commercialism. Thus when it emerged in 1987 that investors in tree-planting were receiving £7 million in grants and tax relief of some £10 million, the forces of environmentalism were mobilized to try to put a stop to it. The tax arrangements devised by the government to encourage forestry were branded as 'concessions', which was debatable, or even as 'fiddles', which they most certainly were not, and conservationists bombarded the media with scandalous stories of rich people investing in trees for the sole purpose of reducing their tax liabilities. The hyperbole of this campaign was exemplified in the London *Evening Standard*, a paper with a largely urban readership, mind you, which bitterly attacked 'the tax-break which allowed the super-rich to wreck the country landscape of Britain by planting thousands of tightly-packed, loss-making conifers all over it'. Almost foaming at the mouth, the paper went on to condemn the government's target of a further 80,000 acres of trees in the uplands of Scotland and Wales, ranted once more about 'alien, sinister conifers' as if they were some malevolent life-form from outer space, and finally demanded the abolition of the Forestry Commission.

The voice of the unthinking country-lover was raised even louder in what became an environmental *cause célèbre*, the battle of the Flow Country. This wild and inhospitable expanse of bog, covering 1500 square miles of northern Scotland, is home to a few hard-pressed crofters and a wide variety of wading birds. It has been described as the largest remaining blanket bog in the world, and naturally engages the interest of the Nature Conservancy Council and many other organizations concerned with wildlife. Not surprisingly, therefore, environmentalist alarm bells began to ring when a company called Fountain Forestry began buying land in the area and applying perfectly legitimately for the government's tree-planting grants. By the beginning of 1987, Fountain had acquired 40,000 hectares and had planted 12,000 of them. In July that year, the Nature Conservancy Council produced a report claiming that the plantations were a threat to birdlife and seeking a moratorium on further afforestation. By means of careful manipulation of the media, the threat perceived by the Council was exaggerated into an ecological disaster and public indignation was assiduously whipped up, especially against the 'tax dodgers' who were alleged to be profiting from this destruction. As a result, in March 1988 the Chancellor of the Exchequer announced in his Budget that the tax arrangements for the planting and management of private forestry were to be removed. 'I hope', said a Scottish representative of Friends of the Earth, 'that we have now seen the end of investment forestry in Scotland by absentee investors.'

As is so often the case with rural matters, what were missing in this 'battle' were a few basic facts. Fountain Forestry's 40,000 hectares sounded an enormous amount in the mouths of the critics: it was precisely 154.375 square miles, or a fraction more than 10 per cent of the Flow Country. The area actually planted by the company covered just 4.63 square miles. According to the trade association of forestry, Timber Growers UK, the optimum area for planting in the Flow Country, in economic terms, would be

100,000 hectares, which is about 386 square miles, or a little more than a third of the area. Obviously, this would affect the bird population. Some species, as foresters claim, would in fact be attracted, but some waders would be forced out. Against this loss must be set the estimate that forestry and associated operations would create two thousand new jobs in northern Scotland during the next twenty years or so, and that, given the nature of the land and the climate, timber is the only hope of such an investment. That part of Britain has an unemployment rate varying locally from 12 to 16 per cent. Scotland as a whole has been experiencing a steady and growing population loss for the past twenty-five years or more – in 1986–7 alone, more than 17,000 people left. Does it make sense to abandon almost fifteen hundred square miles of the country to the birds?

To the ecologists' dismay, the government has taken away from the foresters with one hand only to give back, at least partly, with the other. While the tax incentives have gone, planting grants were increased in 1988, doubled in the case of the environmentally favoured broadleaves, raised by two and a half times for 'alien' conifers. This is a step in the right direction, but more needs to be done if surplus land is to be put to sensible and productive use. So far as forestry is concerned, the Farm Woodland Scheme should be made as attractive to farmers as it was previously to 'absentee investors'. The structure of the grant and tax system, which gave no allowance for the actual purchase of land, meant that forestry companies bought in the cheapest and therefore most marginal areas, infuriating their conservationist critics but often taking over holdings that would otherwise have needed large subsidies to be viable in business terms. The money currently used to prop up farmers producing what is not needed in the multiplicity of Severely Disadvantaged Areas, Less Favoured Areas and so on would be better spent on converting that land to meet a greater proportion of our timber needs in the long term. As the Forestry Commission says, 'Softwoods are a renewable resource like any other.' Special attention should be paid to the planting of decidu-ous species, not only for the sake of landscape and ecology but also out of economic self-interest: the market for hardwoods may be smaller, but it still exists. As for the Forestry Commission, the talk now is of a target of 7 million acres of state-owned woodland, but few experts are convinced that is achievable. It is surely up to the government, and the taxpayers, to make sure that such a target can and will be achieved. The prospect of the great European landmass importing timber is no less ridiculous than the sight of it dumping its surplus foodstuffs.

Of course, convincing farmers that timber is a valuable crop like any other must be part of a comprehensive and radical strategy for agriculture as a whole. Most of the estimates covering the amount of land that should be taken out of production are based on present levels of food-crop surpluses. Some of that land could remain under the plough if the work being carried on under the auspices of the Agricultural and Food Research Council and other bodies was taken really seriously. Again, the vast amounts now being more or less wasted in subsidies could be diverted into a more intensive, sustained and, most of all, highly organized programme of research designed to identify markets for new, non-food crops and then to develop them. Instead of being paid to add to the butter, beef and cereal mountains, farmers could receive aid to run their holdings on an experimental basis, with commercial outlets guaranteed for the future.

Rather than relying on the revival of fifty-year-old technology to get us out of trouble, we should be looking to the techniques of the twenty-first century. One of the most positive areas of agricultural research is in the development of genetically engineered crops that will 'fix' their own nitrogen from the atmosphere, thus removing the need for the artificial fertilizers that are currently causing so much concern. Other strains can be produced that will obviate the use of the even more harmful weedkillers and pesticides, and scientists can also have an important effect on the health aspects of the national diet by helping farmers, as I indicated earlier, to raise leaner animals for meat, or alternative sources of protein, or vegetables richer in vitamins. For the food industry as a whole, crops could be tailored more specifically to the requirements of handling, preparation and presentation, thus helping to keep down costs and consequently prices in the shops.

Above all, however, agriculture should once again be placed on a business footing and not continue to be reliant on the generally unreliable forecasts of politicians and civil servants. Some enterprising farmers have already added food preparation or processing facilities to their holdings, while others have benefited from the study and practice of modern techniques in marketing their produce. It is a trend that should be encouraged more actively than the policies outlined by the Ministry of Agriculture suggest. Instead of intervention boards, we should have large, professional farmers' co-operatives to organize and supervise not so much the growing of crops as the selling of them on a national and international scale. Such organizations would be able to negotiate prices with big buyers from the food processing and retailing sectors and to identify new markets or gaps in existing ones. They might even expand to become processors or retailers themselves, introducing more choice for the consumer and also helping to keep prices stable because of the automatic advantage they would have with their sources of supply. They would be able to work with our European partners on a commercial rather than the existing unsatisfactory political level in order to encourage the right degree of competition and discourage over-concentration on products likely to go seriously into surplus; and where excess production did occur the co-operatives would have pressing economic reasons for disposing of them in a businesslike manner, rather than hoarding them in cold stores.

If this sounds unrealistic, it is no more so than the exercises in deregulation being applied to all sorts of industries, not only in what we like to call the 'free' world but also in the formerly strictly planned economies of Eastern Europe, where after years of largely unsuccessful state control private enterprise has recently begun to receive encouragement. There are international political considerations, too. Progress on developing the system of world trade has been seriously delayed by alleged distortions in markets arising from the levels of subsidy supporting some 12 million farmers throughout the European Community.

Stripped of all the sentimentality and spurious olde worlde charm, farming is a business like any other and, just as any other business, it must adapt as the world changes. It may be argued that it has reached its present state of crisis as a direct result of forty years of continuing refusal to change the way agriculture is organized, in spite of mounting evidence that the structure was obsolete. Farmers themselves are partly to blame for the way in which they have clung to the system of subsidies, but far more blame attaches to governments for their slavish retention of the system, which may have bought them large numbers of votes but has also helped to deprive agriculture of the confidence needed for it to make its own way in the world.

Inevitably, any process of change is likely to be painful, and the radical reshaping required in farming may well hurt more than most, given the years of artificial aid it has received. Yet in spite of what many have seen as undue protection, there have already been significant changes in the structure of agriculture. The number of farms has declined and, more noticeably, so has the number of people employed. As an example, one farm that thirty years ago employed eighteen men on two thousand acres now produces on three thousand acres with just six workers. Indeed, only about 40 per cent of the holdings in Britain now employ outside labour at all and in the past ten years the workforce has been reduced by nearly 75,000, so that farming today accounts for just about 15 per cent of rural employment (except in Northern Ireland, where the figure is 40 per cent). What has been resisted so far is a similar wholesale shedding of farmers themselves, but there seems to be little doubt that the number of holdings will be reduced and it is surely sensible to achieve this by planned withdrawal rather than the present, thoroughly unsatisfactory process of attrition.

One solution might be to buy out farmers approaching an age at which they might wish to retire, or who are in financial difficulties or heavily burdened with debt. Their land could be taken into public ownership and used for a purpose to be decided upon by the local community, or sold on to the outdoor leisure industry, or bought as nature reserves by conservationists prepared to put their money where their mouths are and to raise funds through chari-table organizations dedicated to specific districts. This last would be particularly suitable in the most marginal areas, where grant aid is most expensive, and which could be returned to a state approaching that of genuine wilderness.

The kind of thing that can be achieved to the satisfaction of the environmentalists and the benefit of farmers was demonstrated in 1987 by the Nature Conservancy Council, an official body financed by the government. A farmer leasing 1800 acres in the Isle of Sheppey from the University Chest, which controls land owned by Oxford University, was paid £1.6 million by the Council to turn most of his holding into a nature reserve. The farmer had intended to drain marshland in order to create huge wheatfields (the region holds the world growing record for the crop), but because the land formed part of an official Site of Special Scientific Interest, as a habitat for rare plants and worms and an overwintering ground for huge numbers of wildfowl and waders, he was obliged to negotiate with the Nature Conservancy Council. The Council agreed to pay the farmer a rate set by the district valuer for each year since the start of his tenancy during which he had not used the land for cereal production: it worked out at nearly £325,000 a year. In all, farmers throughout the United Kingdom received £7 million worth of compensation in 1987 for not farming on similar sites.

The drawback to such a scheme is, of course, that it follows the pattern of agriculture soaking up public money. Yet in the words of the Sheppey farmer, Phillip Merricks, 'This is still cheaper to the taxpayer than the paying out for the farm drainage grants and the CAP subsidies that were in force when we started negotiating in 1980.' Nor is there any need for the contributions of taxpayers on behalf of wildlife to be open-ended. Merricks used the £1.6 million he received to set up his own charitable conservation trust for the purpose of managing the marshland.

In the case of other surplus land, some could and should be sold for development, provided that the planning system can be rationalized and the myth laid to rest that the whole countryside is about to disappear under an avalanche of concrete and brick. Whatever the arguments about development – and they are discussed in detail in a later chapter – there is no getting away from the fact that in a country with a population of 56 million, four-fifths of its people are crammed into one-fifth of its land area.

The government recognized this anomaly in 1987 when, in a fairly dramatic shift of policy, the Ministry of Agriculture abandoned its automatic right to be consulted about any non-agricultural planning application covering farmland of more than ten acres. Under a new arrangement, the Ministry agreed with the Department of the Environment that it need only be consulted where planning permission was sought for more than 50 acres of land designated grades one and two, equalling about 17 per cent of the total devoted to farming. Despite the anxieties of conservationists, preservationists, traditionalists and the burgeoning 'heritage' industry, properly controlled and planned development would, for a nation that perceives itself to be overcrowded, be a sensible way of using unwanted farmland. It would also provide a highly profitable exit for some farmers, given that a farm in the South-East, barely breaking even and worth, say, £200,000, would fetch up to a quarter of a million pounds an acre were it to be put on the market as building land.

The essential truth to be faced is that farming as it has been understood – or rather, misunderstood – for the past forty years has had its day. 'Farming is a way of life,' as the American economist William Peterson put it, 'but so was the village blacksmith.' There is no reason why the farmer, any more than anyone else, should be subject to a lifetime guarantee of employment. Agriculture, after all, is about change: changing weather, changing seasons, changing crops, changing states of existence from seedtime to harvest. In order to have a healthy and truly efficient agricultural industry, farmers must be allowed to make money in their own way and on their own terms. Obviously any government is going to want to ensure adequate food supplies for the people it represents, and to have some means of determining the quality and safety of that food, but the level of official interference and regulation should be minimal. In a freer market, of course, some farmers will not make money and they will have to face the consequences, just as the agricultural workers who have lost their jobs had to face the consequences of greater mechanization and other changes in technique and practice.

Given the policies pursued since the 'Dig for Victory' days, it is incumbent upon governments to do what they can in reducing the negative effects of restructuring that they have been largely responsible for delaying too long, but once that obligation has been discharged, generously it is to be hoped, the state must retreat and give agriculture the opportunity to thrive. Farming is hard, risky and sometimes dangerous enough, without having the added burden of a heavy official hand on its shoulder. Morale among farmers is generally so low at present that almost anything which would free them from the bureaucratic muddle that besets them could only improve it. Many farmers themselves argue that the only long-term solution to the present crisis in agriculture is a break with government subsidy. They point out that 80 per cent of the subsidized supplies under the CAP come from the largest 20 per cent of farms, so that smaller holdings lose out anyway. In a system administered by bureaucrats, it is said, farmers never know what prices they are going to get, and what is worse, according to an official of the National Farmers Union, is that after forty years of being insulated from the marketplace by government, 'farmers no longer know what their customers want'.

Some go so far as to suggest that farmers need almost to relearn their trade, so that agriculture is consumer-led rather than technology-driven. That would shift the emphasis, they say, from quantity to quality, and while food prices would probably rise, growing public concern over the health and safety aspects of food would lead to a willingness to pay a little more for better products. Subsidies may have to remain in the short term to help farmers redirect their efforts, according to this line of thinking, but ultimately they will have to go. One way of moving towards that happy day was suggested in 1989 by the International Agricultural Trade Research Consortium, which proposed the replacement of price guarantees by what is called production entitlement guarantees. Each farm would be given a limited price support on a sliding scale that would mean the largest receiving guarantees on only a tiny percentage of their output, with the rest being left to the free market. That way, the Consortium argues, smaller farmers would get a fairer deal and all farmers would base their production on market conditions, since the entitlements would be directed at particular holdings rather than specific crops.

As a solution, it may not be perfect, but it would certainly help to ease the pain of returning agriculture to the marketplace, of giving farming back to the farmers. More important, perhaps, is that it would be a step forward rather than backward, and the crying need is to introduce a new, forward-looking spirit into the most obvious manifestation of rural life. Then perhaps it will be possible to cast aside the romantic fancies, to think clearly and to plan sensibly for a dynamic future in the rest of the countryside.

THREE

First in a Village

If you would be known, and not know, vegetate in a village; if you would know, and not be known, live in a city.

Charles Caleb Colton, *Lacon*

The great changes in agriculture during the past forty years, and particularly its decline as a source of employment, have inevitably brought changes in the pattern of rural life. The sort of transformation that will be necessary, and indeed desirable, for the future of farming as an economic enterprise will mean that the use of the countryside for residential purposes will alter even more.

The beginnings of this process have been obvious for some time – a gradual rise in migration from urban areas, a buoyant market in retirement homes and holiday cottages, for example. In 1987 the predominantly rural counties of East Anglia (that is, Cambridgeshire, Norfolk and Suffolk), which at eighty people per square mile had the lowest population density in England, nevertheless formed the fastest growing region in Britain, with a population increase of more than 500,000 over five years, or 5.1 per cent. The South-West (Cornwall, Devon, Somerset, Avon, Dorset, Wiltshire and Gloucestershire) recorded an influx of 83,000 people from the South-East in 1986 alone, and in the county of Dorset the five-year rate of population increase, at 6.6 per cent, was even higher than the East Anglian average, though that for the region as a whole was lower.

The practical reasons for this population drift from town to country, which has been noted in varying degrees in many parts of Britain, including Northern Ireland, are not difficult to identify. The nature of the migration, however, and its demographic, social and economic effects have been little considered, except at local level in areas where a negative impact has been most marked. That

61

is because practicality is not always the main motivation for moving to the country. The great British rural myth has its part to play, too.

A number of things has contributed to the popularity of rural migration and has influenced its composition. In the 1970s there was a fashion for 'opting out of the rat-race', for buying farms and smallholdings in, say, Suffolk or Wales, and following the cult of self-sufficiency. Some people do still move on the basis of that particular dream, but it is by no means the force that it once was. Apart from the fact that self-sufficiency is almost impossible to achieve, is extremely risky and usually involves a great deal of hard and thankless manual labour, the rat-race became respectable in the 1980s. Paradoxically, this increased rather than reduced the desire to resettle in rural bliss and made the fulfilment of the wish more possible, with consequences for the countryside that are only vaguely understood.

The self-sufficiency fad produced migrants who intended to make ruralism the foundation of their entire lives; the new generation of ruralists, though, often sees the countryside as nothing more than a place in which to have a house. The provision of fast, main-line rail services to places such as Swindon, Norwich, Bristol, Grantham and even York and Doncaster has meant that daily commuting from formerly rather remote rural areas to work in London has become a practical, if expensive, undertaking. Services from provincial airports have also improved – it takes just thirty minutes to fly from Teesside to Heathrow, with a wide choice of flights each day and prices that can compare favourably with those of British Rail. The extension of the motorway network, though still inadequate, and the maintenance of the most liberal tax regime for company cars in Europe make more people more mobile at less expense (more than half of all the new cars sold in Britain each year go to company fleets). All this, combined with the perception of rising affluence among substantial sections of the working population, has offered the possibility of turning a sort of rural idyll into a reality.

The London property boom of the mid-1980s also acted as an incentive to rural migration. People soon discovered that the selling price of a city flat or suburban semi-detached house would buy them a large cottage with extensive grounds and would also pay for refurbishment. Between 1976 and 1986, the total number of property renovations carried out annually in East Anglia rose from 3800 to 9900, half the latter accounted for by owner-occupiers. In the South-West the change was even more striking, with renovations rising from 8000 to 22,300, though just under half the 1986 figure comprised local authority and new-town refurbishment. Alternatively, where building was permitted in rural areas, city-dwellers could buy a new house on a rather grander scale than would have been affordable in London. The average price of new housing in London in 1986 was £56,000, £13,000 more than in East Anglia and the South-West, and up to £20,000 more than in the Midlands and further north. During that same year, the percentage of mortgage advances over the tax-relief limit of £30,000 was 65 per cent in Greater London, against 20 per cent in East Anglia and 22 per cent in the South-West, while the proportion of the purchase price advanced was about the same in all three cases. The economic justification for moving out was obvious.

Then there have been qualitative considerations. East Anglia and the South-West, for instance, have the lowest crime rates in England and Wales, which may have something to do with the fact that, along with the South-East and East Midlands, they share the lowest unemployment rates. The level of domestic expenditure is high in East Anglia and the South-West, indicating healthy disposable incomes; food prices are relatively low; well over half of all houses are occupied by their owners, who have more cars per head than in other parts of the country. Overall, life looks rosy with roses round the door.

It is the quality of life in these two regions that attracts another sort of immigrant: retired people. At 21 per cent, the proportion of the population over retirement age in the South-West is the highest of any regional average in the country, with Dorset the most sought-after location. East Anglia has almost as many, 19 per cent, of men and women aged over sixty-five and sixty respectively, and the proportion is higher than the national average in other predominantly rural and relatively unpopulated areas, such as

Dyfed (20 per cent), Gwynedd (21 per cent), North Yorkshire (19 per cent), the Isle of Wight (25 per cent), Sussex (25 per cent) and the Scottish Borders (21 per cent). Though the South Coast continues to feature the highest concentration of elderly people in the country, rural areas with somewhat less kind climates have risen to challenge it, and forecasts suggest that trend will continue. Again, high property prices in Greater London and the South-East allowed people to sell up on retirement, to buy their dream cottages in the country and to live comfortably on the remaining profit.

Looking at these dry statistics in more human terms, we can see that migration to the countryside has two main elements: relatively well-off commuters and comparatively well-off retired people. These parallel streams of incomers bring with them profound implications for rural areas, particularly at a time when, with agricultural land in surplus, the emphasis has been placed on 'protecting' the countryside rather than developing it. The attitude of the new classes of country folk is crucial, and in 1989 the signs did not appear to be encouraging. What they are doing, for the most part, is attempting to buy a fantasy of country life, but, as one commentator has pointed out in a BBC television programme about East Anglia, 'The rural idyll cannot be bought because in the very act of purchase the hammer falls on real rural life.'

I have already mentioned some of the economic considerations and qualitative judgements that attract newcomers to the country-side, but what is it that ultimately influences their decision? Many are in their thirties and forties, have done well in their careers and have fairly young children. The children are often cited in justi-fication for a move to the country: the lack of amenities – playgrounds, cinemas, nursery schools and so on – is more than compensated for by extra space in the house and, in very many cases, land surrounding the house in which children can play safely and unattended. As a place for indulging in outdoor games, there is no contest between a field and a London street. Space in general seems to be an important factor: many families say they moved because in London they had four bedrooms whereas in, say, Buckinghamshire, they could afford a house with five, or they gained a reception room. This frequently turns out to be important not because they intend to have more children but because they need space to accommodate visitors from town. As newcomers to a village with a small and tightly-knit population, they depend for their main social contacts very often on weekend visits by friends from their former urban area or from work. A certain social cachet has become attached to living in a place where visitors can occasionally swap high-heels or city slip-ons for wellington boots, and it is no longer only the town-based offspring of the landed gentry who find that a Barbour in the wardrobe is *de rigueur*.

A sense of going back to the land seems also to influence many migrants, even if it has been many centuries since the land figured in their lineage. Self-sufficiency, as I said, is not the desirable aim it used to be, but the pleasure of pulling up one's own carrots, digging up one's own potatoes or picking home-grown French beans remains remarkably seductive, in spite of the fact that it is often cheaper to buy such products in a supermarket. Of course the modern obsession with 'healthy living' intervenes here, too: apart from the feeling of achievement, gardening offers a form of physical exercise for people who spend much of their lives behind desks or in cars. Proximity to 'nature' also involves animals, with newcomers often keeping sheep (as pets), goats (which also provide 'healthy' milk, cheese and yoghurt) and horses. The horse, in fact, while being more or less redundant for practical purposes in the Britain of the late twentieth century, has acquired an astonishing degree of popularity, to the extent that a number of new riding magazines has appeared and television offers instruction in such arcane equestrian matters as the niceties of dressage. Playing the countryman – like spending weekends pretending to be old seadogs – seems to satisfy some basic psychological need in the English: not only hearts of oak, perhaps, but hearts of yokels.

Playing and pretending, in truth, is precisely what a great many of the new ruralists are doing, particularly in areas close to cities, and specifically London. The men most often have well-paid jobs in the urban centres, so they are at home only in the evenings and at weekends, working off the frustrations arising from trains that do not run on time (and frequently not at all) or from overcrowded motorways and increasingly congested country roads. The women are sometimes isolated and lonely, their existences dictated by the needs of children (who may offer the only conversation they hear all day) and circumscribed by what can be a lot of driving to take those children to and from school – at least one woman has been recorded as clocking up seventy miles a day in this endeavour. There may be more driving, too, in order to buy food. The day of the old-style village shop that stocked everything is pretty well gone in most small places and buying for a family can be a tiring and time-consuming business, especially in the most attractive market towns which are inundated with tourists from Easter to August Bank Holiday.

As children grow, the pressures increase. For five-year-olds there may be no greater joy than living in the countryside surrounded by unlimited play-space and interesting sights, sounds and animals. But when those children are fifteen, perhaps travelling two hours a day to the nearest secondary school, the story can be very different. Peter wants to go to the cinema, which is miles away, while Jane's friends have asked her to a disco in a different town, and as well as being taken, both have to be brought home again. For a teenager whose family life is essentially an urban one in a rural setting, as opposed to a youngster whose entire existence is rural, the country-side can be a terribly boring place. The cry of 'But there's nothing to *do*' echoes louder along country lanes than city streets, because in many cases there really is nothing to do. Even young people born and brought up in the country long for some urban excitement. Rural life has its frustrations and stresses, too.

This, of course, is only the negative side of the new ruralism, but I have concentrated on it in order to make three points. The first is that the way of life of many incomers is fundamentally suburban rather than genuinely rural, that is, it is not entirely committed to either town or country. From this comes the second point, which is to do with a marked difference in attitude between those whose lifetime experience and livelihood is in the countryside and the people who come to it largely because it seems a more attractive form of suburb.

Country people in general are endowed with a kind of self-sufficiency that has very little to do with growing vegetables. They are accustomed to organizing their lives on the presumption of fewer services, fewer opportunities and fewer support systems, both personal and public. They rely on their own resources more than the average urbanite, and it is this, rather than any lack of friendliness or warmth, that can make it difficult for the newcomers to get to know their neighbours beyond a greeting in the post office (always assuming there still is one). There is, in a village, usually a strong sense of community and an unlimited willingness to help in emergency or adversity, but country folk are used to being on their own and shifting for themselves and they expect other able-bodied people to do the same. They guard their independence, of which they are proud, and they respect that of others. In consequence there is a significant difference in social terms between town and country: a village is not simply a smaller version of an urban community, and many newcomers fail to appreciate the distinctions.

Often this failure is compounded by the fact that the incomer, clinging to the town for economic and other forms of support, does not really share the concerns of the real villager. His horizons are necessarily wider, his daily experience more varied and also, of course, he may be absent much of the time. Thus we come to the third point, which is that mass urban–rural migration of the type that has become so popular is likely to change the character of country communities, suburbanizing them in a sense, until the distinction between town and country life becomes utterly blurred and the less easily defined, more spiritual rural assets the migrants thought they were acquiring are destroyed by homogeneity. In such circumstances, the whole ethos of living in the country is invalidated. It might explode the rural myth, but it will extinguish much that is positive, too.

Whatever the practical difficulties experienced by the new rural-ists, there remains no shortage of people willing to adapt to them in preference to what they consider the more stressful existence of town and city. The seductive power of green fields and open skies continues to gather strength, and escape from subtopia is becoming, if anything, a more widely cherished ambition. Whereas in the past the city-dweller tended often to look down upon his 'unsophisticated' country cousin, the growing feeling now is that the new ruralists rather have the best of it, and display a greater degree of sophistication than those who remain 'trapped' in urban life. As a result, there is now beginning, it seems, a sort of battle for the heart of the countryside between those who have known and lived in it all their lives and people who have invested a great deal of money on realizing their own special rural dream. The struggle has begun to manifest itself in a number of different ways, all of them founded upon the most immediately obvious consequence of the new ruralism, which is its effect on housing in the countryside.

In a small country such as Britain, dominated by its capital, trends usually begin in London and ripple outwards from the centre, as with a pebble dropped in a pool. This has certainly been true in the property market. Greater affluence among the house-owning classes, an expansion of credit and the perception that property, rather than merely providing somewhere to live, was both a safe investment and a means of climbing the social ladder led to furious activity in the London market and, for a time at least, uncontrolled price increases.

Parallel with this grew the fashion for moving to the country, encouraged by a series of new magazines that not only dedicated themselves to the great rural myth but also developed new country 'styles' ranging from curtain fabrics to cars. Whereas the venerable *Country Life* catered for people who already lived in rural areas, publications with titles such as *Country Living*, *Country Homes and Interiors* and *Country Times and Landscape* tended to 'market' the countryside to town-dwellers with the desire and the money to move. Seeing that there was circulation and advertising revenue available from rural romance, more general magazines also took up the cause and the countryside suddenly became glamorous. As always with such trends, there were commercial interests eager to exploit the new ruralism, and leading them were the estate agents, anxious to turn the London boom into a nationwide phenomenon. Banks and building societies, keen to increase lending, bought up chains of estate agencies, new offices were opened and some groups began to establish new and separate departments to deal exclusively in country properties. The sort of prices being paid in London ensured a ready supply of potential buyers seeking either to relocate in a rural area or to buy second homes.

Naturally the South-East, being close to where most of the purchasers worked, was affected first. To take a single example, a one-bedroom cottage in an East Sussex village fifty miles from London was sold for £43,000 in the summer of 1986, sold again the following year for £62,000 and placed on the market in the spring of 1988 at an asking price of more than £90,000. That was considered an easy commute (the British Rail station in a nearby town doubled the size of its car park, which a few months later was full by eight-thirty in the morning), but it was only the beginning. New ruralists in search of better value for money spread to Wiltshire, Lincolnshire, Norfolk and Suffolk (where house prices rose 30 per cent in a year), Wales and even as far as Yorkshire. In popular East Anglia, once the cheapest area of England in which to buy a house, three-bedroom detached cottages were selling in 1987 for £150,000 and more, while estate agents seemed unable to pass a derelict barn without itching to attach a 'For Sale' sign to it. The cost of building land, which had doubled in the South-East in five years, trebled in East Anglia and the South-West and rose by two and a half times in rural areas of the Home Counties.

None of this troubled commuters or weekenders from London, where in some districts selling prices were rising at 20 per cent a month, but it presented serious difficulties for established rural residents wishing to move and in particular for young people seeking a first home. This led to resentment among local people in villages with large numbers of incomers, and the financial aspects of the migration were only part of their concern. With the rising generation of native villagers forced to leave in order to find somewhere affordable to live, the continuity of rural life was being disrupted, the character of villages was changing and the pattern of settlement was being seriously distorted. One East Anglian woman, whose family had lived in or near a particular village for many generations, commented that whereas the traditional rural community had always grown slowly, with a mixture of houses and social classes, whole areas were now changing within a matter of months and the communal structure was being destroyed because high prices meant that houses were available only to a limited group of people. Or as an incomer put it with spectacular disdain: 'People can now afford to live in the country without having to be farm labourers.' Indeed, farm labourers are the very people who will soon be unable to afford living in the country, other than in tied cottages.

In essence, what has happened is that an entire new class of countryman has been created, a new squirearchy with opinions and privileges different from the old but, for financial reasons, equally exclusive. Whatever its faults, the traditional squirearchy was an integral part of the countryside and made its living from it. The new élite comprises mainly the urban professional and executive classes, or self-employed businessmen, or retired people from among those groups. Its members have chosen to live in the country for reasons that have less to do with practicality than with psychology. 'They are buying an image,' said a long-time village resident, to which Brian McLaughlin, author of an unpublished report entitled *Deprivation in Rural Areas*, added: 'Incomers don't understand people who spend all their lives living and working in the countryside.'

The fact is that the new squirearchy in general has no interest in understanding, and thus not much sympathy for, the people whose whole existence is governed by the countryside. It has invested large amounts of its wealth not in a new way of life but merely in a new and more attractive landscape; the way of life remains fundamentally urban, because it is most often from the town that it draws its sustenance. For the most part, the concerns that bring such people to the countryside are basically urban perceptions, as I have already suggested, and along with them comes a set of attitudes – prejudices might be a better word – towards rural life which have been forged in towns, tempered by memory and burnished by nostalgia and sentiment. The countryside is not a community, not an organism, but simply a place, so that the prime concern is not people but surroundings, the chief pleasure is not social but scenic. Such attitudes are hardened by the fact that the rural idyll does not come cheap. Newcomers feel they must protect their investment, so demand must remain well ahead of supply, and at the same time nothing must be done that might tarnish its appeal to others with similar attitudes, since they have become the only ones who can afford to buy. Exclusivity is thus both necessary and inevitable.

One of the first effects all this has on a village is to arrest development, except when it accords with the desires of the newcomers. The new squirearchy tends to oppose anything that will interfere with its vision of the countryside it has bought. Many social agencies have become concerned at the extent of unemployment, poverty and deprivation in rural areas, but attempts to address these problems frequently meet resistance from newcomers whose very presence indicates that they do not share them. The provision of low-cost housing to mitigate the effects on less well-off people of soaring prices is considered a priority by groups such as the Association of District Councils, yet there are many cases where plans to build such houses have brought fierce objections from the new squirearchy. 'It would change the character of the village,' they cry, quite oblivious of the fact that they have already done exactly that. I even heard it seriously suggested by one incomer that village people who could not afford to buy their own homes there should move to a town and 'work their way up the property ladder' until they could afford to move back to the village. The implications of that view are staggering. Are we to have a society in which the poor are to be crowded in inferior housing in run-down cities while living in the country is to be a privilege of the rich?

Similar attitudes prevail with regard to the creation of new forms of employment in rural areas. The new squirearchy sees factories and workshops as having no part in the rural life it is building. Again, people who need jobs are free to go and look for them in towns. The 'character' of the countryside must be protected, even at the cost, apparently, of depopulating it of anyone who earns less than £30,000 a year.

The future of rural areas will be bleak indeed if this new and insidious form of class prejudice is allowed to flourish. The negative effects were summarized by an eighty-year-old Wiltshire man born and bred in a village that is gradually being taken over by newcomers and weekenders. 'There's no life in the village,' he said.

'Young people can't afford to live in it. It's a village for elderly people and weekenders. They aren't much good to the village. Some of them want it tied up in a box for posterity.' People who retire to the countryside do so in search of tranquillity and stability. They see rural life as a fixed point in a world changing ever more rapidly, confusingly and sometimes dangerously, therefore they often resent developments that would benefit those who need to earn a living because change is what they seek to avoid. Yet in the very act of migration such people may be contributing to the decline of the vision of rural life they wish to protect.

When elderly people buy cottages, they obviously become unavailable to younger people, who are obliged to move elsewhere. A decrease in the population of younger people, and especially children, can lead to the closure of a village school, causing disruption and inconvenience to young families who do remain and who themselves may be forced to move out. It is perhaps significant that the South-West, with its high proportion of residents over retirement age, also has the highest number of primary school pupils per teacher in England, in spite of having the lowest percentage of young children. Concentrations of older people in rural areas also place a strain on often sparse medical services, since those over sixty years of age are more likely to require treatment. The South-West, with the second lowest population density in England after East Anglia, recorded in 1986 precisely the national average number of visits to doctors, only 1 per cent lower than in the most densely populated region, the North-West. The figures for the number of hospital cases treated per available bed break down in much the same way, though the North-West had more beds available per thousand of population.

Rural migration by commuters can also act as a disincentive to the provision of better services in country districts. A high rate of car-ownership among incomers – and in the South-West and East Anglia a high percentage of two-car families – tends not to attract better bus services for people who do not own cars, which means about a third of the rural population as a whole. Similarly, the use of cars by newcomers and their continuing urban links may mean that shopping and leisure facilities are not improved for country-dwellers in general, since those with most money to take advantage of them are not inhibited from driving to the nearest town. As I have already mentioned, too, incomers are often able and willing to drive many miles to take their children to school (when they are not boarding, that is), so that even where the juvenile population is increased by their presence the case for providing local schools can be overlooked.

The lack of connection between the growth of interest in the countryside and its development, indeed the obstacles to general improvement that may result from the new and very specific form of migration, have aroused concern among social and welfare agencies and even in the Church of England. In March 1988 the Archbishop of Canterbury, Dr Robert Runcie, announced the establishment on his authority of a Commission for Rural Areas similar to an earlier church inquiry into conditions in the inner cities. The motivation for the inquiry was very clear. 'We believe,' Runcie said, 'the time has come for us to look at our rural inheritance afresh before it slips from our grasp.' Criticizing what he called the widely-held romantic view of life in the country, the archbishop pointed out that village schools, shops, pubs and village halls had been closing at an alarming rate and that while many people seemed to believe that rural life was 'gentle, without problems and hardship', the truth was 'dramatically different'. Deprivation in the countryside was real, although largely hidden because it took place in beautiful surroundings and affected fewer people than in urban areas. The fashion for moving to the country took no account of the difficulties that might be created: 'The social profile of the village has changed out of all recognition.'

There have been signs of resistance to this changing profile among villagers themselves. In some places, houses are no longer advertised for sale, but are passed on quietly, often at below the price that could be expected on the open market, to other long-time residents of the district, especially young people getting married. Some rural families absolutely refuse to sell local property that they inherit, preferring to let it on short leases so that accommodation will be available for their own children when the time comes. It is not unknown in very small villages for newcomers to be approached by neighbours, or even the chairman of the parish council, and interrogated about their degree of commitment to the area, with their welcome or otherwise dependent upon their answers. There have even been cases of villagers objecting to developments that would benefit them, such as the provision of a shop or café, on the ground that they might attract more people than is considered desirable, and some places deliberately deter tourists by such means as unofficially limiting parking space.

The most extreme reaction has arisen in Wales, where a mysterious group calling itself Meibion Glyndwr (Sons of Glendower, the fourteenth-century Welsh hero) has turned its attention from burning down English-owned holiday cottages to fire-bombing estate agents selling Welsh properties in Liverpool, Chester and London. While such tactics are not openly supported by the population at large, residents in certain parts of Welsh-speaking North Wales have made it plain that they do strongly resent not only weekenders but also English people who wish to settle permanently in the region. Significantly, in 1989 North Wales remained one of the chief areas in which house prices continued to rise, while elsewhere the property boom appeared to have run its course.

Yet it is too easy to blame incomers entirely for the battle lines that are apparently being drawn in the countryside. For years many rural areas have existed in an atmosphere of decline in employment, services and population. Now, it seems, they are objecting to an influx of people because those arriving do not conform to the traditional picture of the countryman. As one writer on rural life put it: 'We complain if our villages are emptied of young people and we complain if they are filled up with new ones; we complain if new businesses arrive on our doorstep and we complain if our young people cannot find or create work. We complain about traffic coming through our peaceful lanes and we complain if we are cut off from civilisation because our roads lead nowhere.'

Moreover, country cottages do not appear on the market by accident; their availability indicates that someone is moving away or has died, and in either case somebody benefits from their sale. No purpose would be served if they were left empty and decaying and at least in England we are spared the desolate sight of the many roofless shells and abandoned villages to be found in Ireland as a result of old famine and years of emigration. In addition, the quality of rural housing stock may be significantly improved by newcomers with money to spend. If cottages simply change hands among established local residents, with similar incomes and standards of living, they are less likely to be renovated to a state that should be commonly expected in the late twentieth century. A newly-wed farmworker earning £112 a week will inevitably find it more difficult than a business executive to improve his property. Maintaining the 'character' of village life is a poor justification for continuing the unmodernized state in which many rural properties are still found. There is nothing remotely idyllic about rising damp, dry rot, woodworm, ill-fitting windows, inadequate plumbing and drainage and primitive heating.

The other side of the argument, of course, is that people who can afford to modernize cottages are adding value that puts them beyond the financial reach of farmworkers anyway, so that less well-off country people are obliged to move away, to settle for housing below a standard that ought to be considered acceptable, or simply to abandon the idea of owning their own houses. Their situation has been made worse in recent years by the decline in rented accommodation arising from the Conservative government's antipathy towards public-sector housing, a feeling which is shared by many incomers who would not wish to see their cherished green fields, and perhaps the value of their properties, blighted by council housing estates. It has been argued that the solution to these dilemmas lies in the greater use of housing associations to operate shared-ownership schemes, yet this addresses only part of the problem. A key element in the equation is employment. Part of the reason for the influx of commuters, after all, is that they can afford the continually rising cost of daily travel to town, where most of the jobs are. A one-and-a-half-hour commute by train to London from the Home Counties cost about £14 a day in 1988. It is no use providing a manual worker with low-cost rural housing if he then has to spend £70 a week in order to travel to where he can find work.

   As the Countryside Review Committee stated in 1978, a policy for rural areas cannot exist in isolation, and the requirements for serious attempts to revitalize the countryside in what is becoming a post-industrial and, in a sense, also a post-agricultural age are reviewed in a later chapter. Before we even start to consider such things, however, attitudes towards the countryside must be reviewed both among people who have always lived there and new arrivals. Not only must both sides learn to understand each other, but they need also to understand that neither of their sectarian visions of country life will ultimately be beneficial to the areas in which they have, out of habit or choice, made their homes. The rural writer I quoted earlier commented that the countryman's reputation for grumbling to which he referred 'is part of our nature because we do not like change'. That is also part of the nature of the incomers, because their decision to change from town to country is, at bottom, most often conditioned by a desire to escape from change, or at least from its less comfortable effects. But for native and newcomer alike, the countryside has changed and must continue to change, or else it will simply stagnate, and what Archbishop Runcie described as our rural heritage will be lost.

   The first thing is to realize that our rural heritage is not all of a piece, but is infinitely varied and has involved people of all sorts and classes. The emphasis there is on people. One of the striking features of the British landscape is the extent to which it has been formed and settled by people. That process has been continuing for many centuries and to suggest – as do some environmentalists and many country-dwellers, not least the newcomers – that it should simply stop is sheer folly. The countryside was not invented in 1885 or 1912 or 1932 and it cannot somehow be frozen now.

   What many people now think of as the 'traditions' of rural life have been constantly changing, too. Some, it is true, have survived for hundreds of years, even if the reason for them no longer applies or has been forgotten, but others have disappeared, have been overtaken by new circumstances, have been discontinued for lack of interest or have just become irrelevant. How often are village ducking stools or stocks used nowadays? Once they were very much parts of rural life. How many people now entertain dinner guests at three o'clock in the afternoon, as the eighteenth-century Norfolk parson and diarist James Woodforde did, so that visitors might be safely home before dark? That was traditional behaviour before roads were metalled and cleared of footpads. Who now relies for water on the traditional village pump? There is hardly a traditional village shop to be found today, and even the traditional village postmistress is a vanishing breed.

The truth is that traditional rural life, like traditional methods of farming, never existed as any sort of fundamental, unchanging force; they altered and adapted as the rest of the world did under mankind's restless and relentless hand. Were that not true, we would still be living in caves or mud huts surrounded by impenetrable forests. To be sure, there were periods, sometimes long ones, when there was little or no development of rural life, but they have always been followed by technological advances, social and political adjustments and experiment which brought changes in their wake. The land on which I lived in Cambridgeshire, part of the 'traditional' scenery of East Anglia, was actually uninhabited bog until the 1880s, when it was drained and transformed into a striking landscape of fields and dykes, to which farms and houses, roads and railway lines were later added. Indeed, the Victorian period, with its rapid industrialization and vast urbanization programmes, ended the pre-eminence of the countryside in the British social and economic structure and in so doing rendered virtually extinct the real traditions of rural life. What is so casually referred to as being 'traditional' today is nothing more than something we remember or, worse, think we remember, a small part of the past that has lost its way and been seized upon as a floating refuge in a sea of uncertainty swirling round the future. We feel we need something to hold on to, something solid and immutable, and many of us have reached out for the countryside.

But with so much changing about us, we cannot realistically expect the countryside to remain exactly as it is, nor should we blind ourselves to the changes that have already taken place there. What we must do is not attempt to reverse or prevent change, but make the best of it, which in this case means deciding how the countryside and rural life in general are best to be accommodated in the process of change. Moving to the country simply because it is perceived as being 'better' than the town is not positive enough. It does not in itself generally improve conditions in rural areas and it does not relieve the pressure on urban areas – the road and transport systems in London, for instance, are reaching breaking point under the weight of more than a million daily commuters. Seeking to discriminate between residents and newcomers, on the other hand, is not positive at all, and both sides of the divide are guilty of that. The greatest change that must be recognized is that, for perhaps the first time in history, economic factors have affected the only thing that can truly be said to be traditional about the countryside – the distinction between it and the town.

The first sign of this weakening of boundaries came with the virtual merging of urban and rural property markets, which began naturally enough in the South-East and spread during the boom to many other parts of Britain. On early evidence this interaction between urban selling prices and rural buying appears to be a negative development and, if it continues in isolation, it will surely prove to be so. Inflation of rural house prices on no better grounds than a level of demand that has in a way been artificially created will, unless it is somehow checked, fundamentally alter the social structure of the countryside to that of middle-class suburbs, while at the same time adding to the housing problems of the inner cities as less well-off people are forced to move from rural to run-down urban areas in search of property they can afford.

To be sure, there was a recession in London house prices from the late summer of 1988, brought on by a change in arrangements for mortgage tax relief and the government's reliance on high interest rates as a means of combating a rising rate of inflation. This was inevitably followed by stagnation in the property market in some other parts of the country, but overall there was very little change, other than a slight lessening of activity, in the demand for rural properties. By the summer of 1989 estate agents were reporting that the market for houses in the country remained strong almost everywhere, particularly in the North, where Dales cottages with charm, some land and a pretty view – 'what the punters want', to quote a Yorkshire agent – were still selling for

£200,000. There had been some price reductions in East Anglia, but only from the wildly inflated levels of the previous year, while in specific locations prices were still actually rising as a result of road and rail improvements likely to be of benefit to commuters.

The boom appeared to have reached its limit for the time being, but its effects continued to be obvious, and, after all, a reduction in the real value of property in Britain has been virtually unknown since the end of the Second World War. Indeed, the very stabilization of the market could not necessarily be seen as good news for the countryside, especially if all it meant was that prices rose less quickly than had been the case. Newcomers who spent hundreds of thousands of pounds on their rural retreats when the boom was at its peak would be likely to do everything in their power to protect their investments, which would no doubt include resisting any developments – such as the provision of low-cost housing for the less well-off – that they might see as adversely affecting the value of their properties.

In rural areas perhaps more than anywhere else, the lesson of the great property boom was surely that some means of controlling the housing market is socially desirable, as much as anything to ensure that the social mix which has so far characterized the countryside is maintained. One method might be simply to resist urban migration and, by so doing, limit the rise in property prices. The government could, for example, levy capital gains tax on principal residences sold before having been occupied by their owners for five years, unless there were extenuating circumstances or pressing reasons why such sellers had to move. This is the system adopted in France, where the rate of increase in property prices has been held to an average of about 10 per cent a year. Renovation costs are deducted from the capital gains tax liability, encouraging the improvement of property where investment potential is the chief reason for buying.

Abolition of mortgage tax relief for people paying income tax at the top rate would be another way of containing house-price inflation and allowing more lower-paid people, many of whom are to be found in rural areas, to buy their own homes. This would be a logical step in view of the government's aim to 'target' more precisely state aid to individuals and would also help to achieve the desired proportion of owner-occupation above the current 63 per cent. As for second homes and weekend cottages, the prospect of paying double the local rate of community charge, or poll tax, might deter some would-be purchasers, but that in itself is unlikely to help people at present unable to afford a first home, let alone a second.

In fact, while there may be some merit in attempting to limit property speculation by means of taxes, such action would probably do little in itself to counter rural deprivation, being more likely to preserve the status quo than to encourage development and revitalization of the countryside. That might suit people whose chief concern is what they think of as the privileged 'character' of rural life, but for many others preservation would simply mean stagnation. The French rural property market, for example, has begun to betray rising dependence on foreign buyers, particularly in southern areas of high unemployment and in other places which are being depopulated because of a change in fashion towards living in towns.

The second possible line of approach to what must be recognized as a very real problem would be more controversial but perhaps all the better for that. This would be actually to acknowledge that the countryside can benefit from an influx of people and to encourage migration by offering incentives to industry and commerce to follow or even lead the new commuters into rural districts. In compiling the *Decentralisation Report 1988*, the commercial property consultants Jones Lang Wootton discovered that companies employing a total of 36,000 people intended to move out of central London during the next few years. The main reasons for their desire to move were high property costs and rates, but another factor was the rising level of 'London-weighted' salaries, which reflect the higher costs of workers living in or commuting to the capital. Many companies looked no farther than the redeveloped London Docklands, the outer suburbs and the Home Counties, but that trend was changing as many of the drawbacks associated with central location began to arise in areas close to London, too. The government's programme to revitalize inner cities has tended to draw outward-looking companies to urban areas in the North and Midlands; similar financial and practical help could direct them to rural areas.

Of course, this is not as simple as it sounds. Outmoded planning assumptions, which are discussed in Chapter Five, and naked prejudice are serious obstacles to the provision of an employment base in the countryside to replace agriculture. Yet, as I have shown, agriculture must be replaced if country life in any real sense is to survive at all, because farming is one of those rural traditions that is no longer as relevant as it was, and in the case of most people who live in the countryside does not apply at all, beyond determining the landscape visible from their cottage windows. In finding suitable alternatives, the main fear to be overcome is the fear itself. Those who cling to the rural past also seem to keep alive visions of industrial history, forgetting that industry in the late twentieth century does not mean grimy factories and smoke-belching chimneys. Since 1983, very nearly half of the companies that have moved out of London have been in the service sector, with such enterprises as banking and insurance leading the way. All they need are premises, communications and people, none of which is going irreparably to damage the 'traditional' landscape any more than silage towers and prefabricated barns do. Any perceived disadvantage of their appearance would be more than offset by the benefits, the support and social services that would follow and, most of all, the change in attitude of newcomers whose domestic and working lives were combined in a single rural area.

While there would be some acknowledgement of the fusion that has already taken place between town and country, the distinctive qualities of rural life would actually be enhanced because there would be less dependence on the urban areas for the things that are currently lacking in the countryside but that would follow the sort of committed migration I have outlined. There are already examples of this throughout the country, but one known to me personally is of a man who runs an oil business from a remote cottage in Swaledale and, in his spare time, operates a restaurant in the village, thus adding to its facilities and providing at least some employment in a district where little is available.

Service industries by themselves, though, would not represent a revival across the whole range of rural life. The personnel they require are relatively few and specialized, generally salaried rather than wage-earning. Development incentives in the countryside could be offered to industries closely related to farming, such as the expanding food processing and preparation sector. This would not only benefit a restructured agricultural industry, as I suggested in the previous chapter, but would also offer employment to young country-dwellers for whom farmwork is inexorably becoming less and less of an option, as well as helping to maintain and even strengthen the basic link between ruralism and food production, so that the underlying character of the countryside was not completely destroyed and its separation from the urban areas preserved in another way. All industries need support systems, so that the rural economy as a whole would be revived – people, who are the essential component of any way of life, need to be fed, clothed and supplied with the necessities and luxuries of modern society, and the more people there are, the more the sources of those supplies will increase. At the same time, a rural work-force enjoying job security and better pay would be in a stronger position to compete in the local property market, so that migration would be more balanced and a spread of different social classes occupying different types of housing would continue. The simple expedient of establishing local, publicly available registers showing the selling prices of houses would go a long way towards preventing the artificial inflation caused by estate agents 'talking up' properties and creating the sort of panic buying that was a feature of the 1980s boom in country property.

Sensible, integrated and controlled development of the type I have described could not really be said to 'spoil' the countryside, except in terms of the narrow-mindedness, suspicion, snobbery and downright selfishness that characterize so many of the pronouncements which are so often heard about it. The Countryside Review Committee of 1978 itself recognized the fundamental problem:

Often the countryside is thought of as scenery or a place for recreation. Yet for millions of people it is home and livelihood. The social and economic aspects of the countryside are therefore of fundamental importance ... The economic life of all rural communities will be radically affected by developments which government, in the long run, cannot control ... There are no easy general answers. What we can do is analyse, more precisely, the interplay of the principal forces. It is this analysis which, on the whole, has been lacking in the past. Attempts to treat the problems of rural communities have concentrated on particular aspects in isolation, and there has been little attempt to see problems in the round ... a comprehensive approach is the only one to offer any chance of success. Otherwise we may cope with the symptoms but leave the real issue – the interactions of people, functions and activities – unexplored and untouched.

People, functions and activities, with people heading the list. Rural life is not about fields and hedgerows, woods and streams; they are merely the background on which it is drawn. If that is all we want from the countryside, then there is no need for anyone to live there and we might as well all crowd into towns, emerging at weekends to gaze at empty rural vistas from our cars and coaches, visitors to the ultimate in national parks. If it is country life, rather than merely the countryside, that we wish to preserve, then it is to the health and condition of its communities that we must look, not through the distorting mirror of half-remembered or invented history but under the clear lens of present and future needs. The ploughman no longer homeward plods his weary way, as he did in Gray's *Elegy*, and those who wish to keep the countryside forever in his shadow, as well as those who think they can buy some of the life they imagine he led, had better realize it.

For the moment, they have a choice: they can accept sensible, small-scale and appropriate development which, given the desperation of developers to find something to develop, will often include some additional amenity for the community such as a hotel or a golf course, and as a quid pro quo they can insist that an area of woodland be planted or landscaping be undertaken to preserve the rural appearance. But that choice may not be available for ever, for no matter how hard it is resisted, the future will not be stopped, and the development that comes with it could be of an altogether different order. In the south of England in particular, the pressure was only just beginning to be applied seriously in 1988; there was still time to dissipate it and to protect the countryside by sensible co-operation. Already, though, local planning authorities have shown signs of vulnerability to what has been called 'greenmail' – the fear sown by developers that if a current scheme is rejected it will be followed by others less environmentally sensitive and sooner or later one of them will be forced through on a surge of demand.

Ruralism as a way of life has been declining in Britain for centuries and the changes in the economic and social structure wrought by the Agricultural and Industrial Revolutions have ensured that, barring some unforeseen global catastrophe, it can never return in its old form. The modern revival of interest in rural life offers an opportunity to give the countryside a new and vital role; to re-integrate it fully, after years of neglect, into the fabric of economic existence; to free it from its romantic but dead past and lead it towards a perhaps somewhat less romantic but at least a living future. This can only be achieved, however, if the internal dynamics of country life in its fullest sense are maintained and adapted. Houses alone do not make a community, and less so if they are inhabited by people who are absent for much of the time and whose chief contribution is to an economic structure that has no interest in the countryside. In a nation that has far more agricultural land than it can usefully employ and far more crowded cities than its available land justifies, rural migration should be approached as a positive development. It is only negative if, as has happened up to now, it takes place in isolation, without being followed by the benefits of consolidation that movements of population usually involve. The new ruralism will begin to make sense when there has been a significant reduction in the number of property advertisements containing phrases such as 'idyllic setting, 5 miles from M4' and 'beautiful views, 10 mins mainline station, King's Cross 50 mins'.

Before the traditionalists and the new squirearchy come together at the barricades in defence of the great rural myth, they had better be aware of what precisely it is they are fighting for, and they might do well to recall another line from Thomas Gray's poem:

The paths of glory lead but to the grave.

FOUR

The Call of Nature

What would the world be, once bereft
Of wet and wildness? Let them be left,
O let them be left, wildness and wet;
Long live the weeds and the wilderness yet.

Gerard Manley Hopkins, 'Inversnaid'

The two words used most often about the countryside today are 'conservation' and 'heritage'. They, indeed, formed the title of one of the discussion papers produced by the Countryside Review Committee, set up under the auspices of the government in 1974: *Conservation and the Countryside Heritage*, the paper was called. Its starting point, in the committee's own words, was the identification of a new 'conservation ethic'; and the word conservation was interpreted as 'embracing acceptance of necessary change but, at the same time, as seeking to manage and direct it in such a way as to minimise adverse effects and, as far as possible, to preserve vital areas, elements and features of the countryside'. There were, of course, immediate problems with this. What, for example, *were* the vital areas, elements and features of the countryside? Which effects were to be considered adverse? Most important of all, who was to make such judgements?

In the opinion of the review committee, this new conservation ethic implied the recognition of limits to resources and thus that they could no longer be squandered, whether for use or enjoyment. Another implication was that the purpose of conservation was to be positive, not 'merely to prevent and control the unacceptable' and that such an aim required the widest possible co-operation. 'Too often,' the committee said wisely, 'conservation has been seen as simply the preservation of the status quo. On the other hand, change and development have often been insensitive in application. Both approaches are self-defeating. The one because ... change is

89

inevitable. The other when it carries the implicit and untenable assumptions, that change equates with improvement and that there is a virtually unending supply to replace what is lost.'

What the committee failed to address was the attitude that has now become widespread, namely the 'implicit and untenable assumptions' that change – at least in so far as the countryside is concerned – equates with destruction and loss, and that there is a virtually unending supply of things which must be kept.

The committee also failed to offer any working definitions, as opposed to interpretations, of the words it was using, so it may be valuable to return to basics and, with the help of the *Oxford Dictionary*, consider some fundamental meanings. To begin with, the word 'heritage' simply refers to anything that is or may be inherited, or the portion of an inheritance allotted to an individual. The verb 'to conserve' is defined in precisely the same way as 'to preserve' – to keep safe from harm, decay or loss – and might therefore seem redundant, except for an important additional nuance of meaning: 'especially with view to later use'. The adoption of these words in connection with the countryside has, it seems, involved subtle variation of their meanings. 'Conservation' has been stripped of its connection with 'later use' and is taken to mean nothing more than preservation, while the word 'heritage' now carries the unspoken implication that practically anything touched by one's ancestors is not only immutable and somehow holy but also the property of everyone else, too. In the case of the first, the purpose of its use is merely to disguise the true aims of those who espouse it: what they want is not to conserve in the real meaning of the word, but simply to preserve, not to use but merely to keep what they have decided should be kept. The Conservation Bureau of the Scottish Development Office was bold enough to come right out and say it: 'Conservation is defined as "action taken to ensure the survival of something we value" ...'

The distortion of 'heritage', though, is related to a different and more insidious phenomenon, as the cultural historian Robert Hewison detected in his book *The Heritage Industry*:

I call it the 'heritage industry' not only because it absorbs

The real face of modern farming: silage towers and the cheerful untidiness of everyday agricultural life do not accord with the sentimental picture beloved of those who cling to the vision of a pastoral idyll

As overproduction erodes the viability of agriculture and reduces the numbers of farmers who can make a living from it, the options for the future that have emerged so far are not encouraging. Some turn the holdings into fun parks, others try 'horseyculture' and B & B, but for many the choice is to sell up

nting country: the wild and beautiful
kshire Dales near Catterick frequently
e as a practice battleground for the
y, and motorists meandering to enjoy
scenery may see more then they bar-
ned for. Meanwhile, in another part of
kshire, the Fylingdales early warning
ion adds a certain something to the view

The countryside in spring early morning at Battle station in East Sussex find recently expanded car pa almost completely full of vehicles left by commute

d much talk of natural
ty, National Park
orities seem unable to
t the temptation to
ify, as with the suitably
c additions to a footpath
g a disused railway line
ow left). At the same
, footpaths in even the
otest areas lose much of
'traditional' character
n road-building
niques are used to repair
ion caused by walkers

The countryside at w
rural life is not all ab
lambs gambolling o
hillsides – the wilde
and most beautiful a
often contain much-
needed natural resou
and quarrying has its
place, too, in the rur
scene

The conservation of
is called 'traditional'
woodland is an impo
part of the work of th
Forestry Commissio
signs such as this one
raise questions: wha
being conserved, wh
and for whom?

l reproduction:
prevailing
ntryside ethic
n means that new
ding is nothing
e than a rather
h imitation of the
The possibilities
houghtful inno-
on are rarely
sidered

udy in contradic-
the Trawsfynydd
ear power station
very noticeable
tion to the
wdonia National
in Wales.
ddled thinking has
confusion about
real purpose of
onal Parks

This reed bed alongside an opencast mine at East Chevington, Northumberland, is designated part of a one hundred acre nature reserve. Exploitation and conservation are not mutually exclusive, and reconstruction is always an option

considerable public and private resources, but also because it is expected more and more to replace the real industry upon which this country's economy depends. Instead of manufacturing goods, we are manufacturing *heritage*, a commodity which nobody seems able to define, but which everybody is eager to sell ... it involves the preservation, indeed reassertion, of social values that the democratic progress of the twentieth century seemed to be doing away with ... If the only new thing we have to offer is an improved version of the past, then today can only be inferior to yesterday ... The urge to preserve as much as we can of the past is understandable, but in the end our current obsessions are entropic: that is to say, as the past solidifies around us, all creative energies are lost.

The heritage industry Hewison describes operates in more urban settings – in the arts, architecture, museums and so on – but its essential features may equally be applied to many of those who presume to campaign on behalf of the countryside. While sometimes paying lip-service to the need for change, they are principally concerned with what Hewison calls solidifying the past around us. The rural scene they value is that of a century and more ago, tinted by the palette of the Victorian watercolourist or, better yet, of Constable, bathed in the sentimental glow of Romantic poetry, heavy with the tranquillity of Gray's *Elegy*.

Worse still, there is about the fashion for conservation/preservation a curious form of animism or even anthropomorphism, a tendency to view human life as no more valuable than that of plants or animals, as if mankind really were nothing more than a naked ape. The emphasis is on the human being as destroyer, the thoughtless exploiter of the natural world who must be stopped in his tracks before he lays waste the entire planet. The countless examples through the centuries of man's ability to copy, recreate, order and improve upon the work of nature are as nothing, and his capacity for continuing to do so in the future is therefore ignored.

But perhaps the most reprehensible aspect of the current concern for the countryside lies in its combination of hypocrisy and muddled thinking. Conservationists, like anyone else, enjoy and benefit from the use of electricity, yet they continually dispute the need for mining, hydro-electric schemes and power stations; they accept the convenience of the car and the aeroplane, yet they repeatedly oppose the building of roads and airports; they appreciate the pleasures of the countryside, yet increasingly they are seeking to restrict the access of others by imposing limits on building in their favoured areas. All this, they claim, arises out of a selfless desire to protect 'the environment', a vague and mysterious place which seems to have acquired in recent years the quality of consecrated ground, particularly in the sense that it has very little to do with living people. But what is this environment that they are protecting?

To remain in the business of definitions for a moment, the environment consists of 'surrounding objects, regions or conditions, especially circumstances *of life of person or society*' (my italics). To the conservationists, however, the environment is no more and no less than what they have decided Britain should look like, notwithstanding the fact that this 'traditional' appearance is largely the result of thousands of years of destruction by our ancestors. They have so distorted history that the depredations of humankind from the Stone Age onwards have taken on the appearance of natural events, through the road and urban building programmes of the Romans, the landscape-altering feudal system of agriculture, the enclosures of the sixteenth and seventeenth centuries that changed the face of most of the countryside, right up to the energetic interference of those great vandals, the Victorians. In the absence of hardly a square mile of Britain left in its truly natural state, the rural heritage industry has chosen the end of the nineteenth century as the point at which to pickle the landscape, so to speak.

The choice may be arbitrary and illogical, yet in a way it is understandable. Britain is a small country with a relatively large population (roughly the same as that of France, which is approximately twice the size), and a long history of what is considered to be civilization. A consequent lack of primeval forest, untouched wilderness and even land that is uninhabited makes it difficult for the conservationist to find something essentially belonging to nature to preserve. Not only does that help to explain Britain's comparatively late entry into the sphere of official conservation but it also provides the perfect framework for conflict between those who place greater value on the past, others whose preoccupation is the requirements of the present and the small number who try to lay firm foundations for the future. Nowhere is this conflict more apparent than in the policies and practices of the British National Parks.

The concept of the national park is an American one. Yellowstone, mostly in the state of Wyoming, was the first such area, inaugurated as long ago as 1872. The idea was that unclaimed wilderness should be the property of the nation, for the benefit of the population as a whole and as a means of preserving some of the striking natural features of landscape, flora and fauna free of human interference, except in the provision of benign management. It was not until 1949 that similar ideals were officially adopted in Britain, following a report four years earlier by an architect and naturalist named John Dower and, in 1947, the recommendations of a committee convened to consider how national parks might best be administered. These two reports formed the basis of the National Parks and Access to the Countryside Act 1949, which resulted during the 1950s in the establishment of the ten National Parks that now exist in England and Wales. The Welsh Parks are in the Brecon Beacons, Snowdonia and Pembrokeshire, while the English ones cover Dartmoor and Exmoor in the West Country, the Peak District of Derbyshire, the Lake District, the North York Moors, the Yorkshire Dales and part of Northumberland.

No doubt the enthusiasts who helped to bring about the creation of the National Parks – like their present-day successors who manage and support them – were earnest and well-intentioned. On behalf of the conservationists, it must be said that various parts of Britain show in dramatic and sometimes unpleasant fashion what may happen when land is left entirely at the mercy of owners and commercial interests. There is now a general recognition that the careless exploitation of natural resources can have far-reaching effects on ecological stability, many of which are at best undesirable and at worst dangerous. But while in one sense the founders of the

National Parks were visionaries, in another way they displayed remarkable naïvety and lack of imagination. The national park is one of many concepts that have not transferred well across the Atlantic.

An important reason for this is to be found in the fundamental difference between America and Britain. In the United States, the federal government owns about a third of the land area of the country – 740 million acres or rather more than 12 million square miles – and of that total, 10 per cent has been designated as national park. In Britain, with a land area of just 94,250 square miles, public ownership accounts for only 12.6 per cent, and the policy of privatizing public assets that has been followed by the Conservative governments of the 1980s has meant that the trend is downward. For instance, the biggest single landowner in the country, the Forestry Commission, has been obliged, under government pressure, to begin the process of selling something like 10 per cent of its 2,878,758 acres into private ownership. So while it remains true that the National Parks in Britain, occupying 9 per cent of the total land area, form a greater part of the whole than those in America, only 2 per cent of the 3,359,672 acres designated here as National Park is actually owned by the state (with a statistically insignificant 0.38 per cent more publicly owned for the purpose of wildlife conservation through the Nature Conservancy Council). Thus the government, on behalf of the public, has nothing like the power over land use that is enjoyed by the United States Department of the Interior, which manages 70 per cent of federal land; and, unlike the US National Park Service, the British managers of National Parks do not have absolute control over the land they are charged with supervising: nearly all of it belongs to somebody else.

There is a further important difference between American and British national parks. In the United States, the wilderness areas so designated are just that – virtually unpopulated wildernesses. (People were actually moved out of some areas when certain parks were designated.) In Britain the National Parks contain not only working farms, but also mines, quarries, hydro-electric schemes, military firing ranges, an oil terminal in one case, villages and even quite large towns. The little Dartmoor National Park (365 square miles), for example, had a human population of 30,000 when the national census was taken in 1981, and it includes the town of Ashburton, with a population of almost 4000. The population of the town of Brecon, in the Brecon Beacons (519 square miles of National Park), is closer to 8000. The Park also covers the substantial town of Abergavenny, encompasses several main roads and has a total population of 32,000. Farther north, the Snowdonia Park contains, of all things, the Trawsfynydd nuclear power station, as well as some fairly large and busy settlements, while in the North York Moors one of the striking landmarks is the Fylingdales early warning radar station operated by the Ministry of Defence. Some of the Parks were never wildernesses, and none can be described as such now. Paradoxically, the small amount of wilderness remaining in Britain is almost all to be found in Scotland, which has not a single National Park.

Unlike the American version, then, the British National Park is not at all what its name suggests: it is not national, because it is overwhelmingly privately owned, and it is not a park in any commonly accepted meaning of the word, because people live and work in it and the land is expected, to a greater or lesser degree, to earn its keep. Nor are the aims of the National Parks as easy to achieve in Britain as they are in the federally owned wildernesses of America. Indeed, the aims themselves are inherently conflicting. According to Sir Derek Barber, chairman of the Countryside Commission, which has overall responsibility for the Parks, they were established so that 'the best of our countryside should be recognised and protected, the way of life therein sustained, and public access for open-air recreation encouraged'. But the way of life may well depend on not protecting the countryside in the way the conservationists would wish, and I know from personal experience of living in the Yorkshire Dales National Park that both life and landscape can be seriously disturbed by the encouragement of access by the public for open-air recreation.

As a result, the National Park authorities are criticized from all sides. Conservation groups attack them for failing to give adequate protection to the countryside; organizations representing leisure interests complain that public access is all too often restricted or forbidden; people who live in the Parks chafe under what seem to them petty bureaucratic rules and procedures that may prevent them from improving their houses as they would wish – like the man who was ordered to demolish an extension because it was a few inches higher than regulations allowed. The authorities most often find themselves in a defensive posture, falling back on what is undoubtedly the truth, that they do not have enough money to carry out their functions properly. At £13 million in 1987–8, the funds provided by the government for the ten National Parks were rather less than the grant given to support the Royal Opera House, Covent Garden. For the following year, the grant was reduced to £10.93 million, in spite of the fact that what amounted to an eleventh Park, though not actually designated as such, was created to repair the damage caused by years of neglect and rampant tourism in the Norfolk and Suffolk Broads.

Only two Parks, the Lake District and the Peak District, have their own independent planning boards and set their own budgets. The rest are administered by committees of the county councils in whose areas the Parks have been created. This sometimes serves only to increase the difficulties of maintaining a balance between local and national interests. The Yorkshire Dales, which for 1988–9 received the largest grant, £1,031,850, of any National Park, is sited mostly in the county of North Yorkshire and partly in Cumbria, so the committee that manages it comprises twelve Yorkshire councillors and one from Cumbria. In addition there are three members from district councils in the area, such as Richmondshire, and eight members appointed by the Secretary of State for the Environment on account of their special expertise or interest in matters affecting the Park. In effect, seven-eighths of the Park's budget comes from the government, though the details are not quite as simple as that. Three-quarters of the resources come directly from the Department of the Environment on the basis of advice by the Countryside Commission. The remaining quarter of the financing comes from North Yorkshire and Cumbria county councils in the ratio of seven to one, but since half of all local government finance is provided by the national government, only about an eighth of the money granted to the Park is raised directly from the ratepayers who actually live in the area.

In a way, this is as it should be, for it is hard to see the Park as being operated, in strictly practical terms, for the benefit of its inhabitants as much as for that of the ten million people who visit the Yorkshire Dales each year. Locals do not need such things as information centres and signs showing them where footpaths are. Yet this minimal direct local connection also means that many residents do not feel much involved with the work of the Park, often seeing it as something imposed from above and resenting it when it interferes with their everyday activities. Thus the Park tends automatically to be classified as something negative, which means that it starts in the position of having to defend itself.

As defined by the Park officer for the Yorkshire Dales, Richard Harvey, the responsibilities of the National Park authority are conservation, planning, 'information and interpretation', recreation, support for the local community and management and administration. In detail as in outline, therefore, the situation is rich in potential for disagreement and confrontation. The Park justifies its activities on various grounds, all of them arguable. The neat and rather twee wooden signs indicating footpaths and beauty spots are, it is claimed, for the purpose of ensuring that visitors do not trespass, yet it can hardly be said that they enhance the landscape. The sometimes rather ugly Visitor Centres are presented as offering opportunities for tourists to understand local ways, but the great mass of visitors are not renowned for their understanding or even interest, while the majority of the locals simply want to be left alone to pursue their ways in peace. Perhaps most tenuously, it is suggested that the presence of a National Park offers a source of local employment – a study in 'job creation' if ever there was one! The Dartmoor Park authority, for example, employs about fifty full-time staff, not a high percentage of a 30,000 population. A couple of strategically placed hypermarkets would certainly provide more jobs.

Even the conservation role claimed for the Parks is sometimes difficult to understand. Again in Dartmoor, the Park authority states openly and officially that the use of land for military purposes is incompatible with the status of the area, yet the Ministry of

Defence has 33,000 acres in the Park dedicated to military training. Much of the land used as army firing ranges is located in an officially designated Site of Special Scientific Interest, which the Park authority admits has been damaged. No action has been taken (and certainly the Park authority is in no position to take any) to resolve this plainly ludicrous situation.

Nor is conservation policy helped by Park authorities' other obligation to encourage tourism. In 1987, while complaining about the insufficiency of its government grant, the Yorkshire Dales pledged itself to spend £750,000 (later reduced to £500,000 because of budget cuts) on repairing the havoc caused by visitors to nearly fifteen miles of moorland footpath classified as severely damaged and a further nineteen miles considered to be in need of immediate restoration work. What better illustration could there be of the fundamental paradox of the national park on the muddled British model?

The first signs of damage were noticed in 1985 in an area of the Pennines known as the Three Peaks: Ingleborough, Whernside and Penyghent. A user survey was undertaken and the reason for the deterioration soon became apparent. Each year the area is the site of the Three Peaks Challenge Walk, which covers twenty-five miles and attracts 15,000 entrants. It is also used for an annual fell race and a cyclo-cross competition. In addition, 150,000 people climb Ingleborough each year – it is one of the best known 'beauty spots' in the Dales; 50,000 make their way up Whernside and a similar number climb Penyghent: that makes a total of more than half a million ruggedly-booted feet tramping over the thin, fragile upland soil. An expert summoned from the Institute of Terrestrial Ecology described the scene as the worst footpath erosion he had found anywhere in the country. Most of the paths had become nothing more than boggy tracks and in some places had been trampled to nearly 40 feet wide (one was found to be no less than 450 feet across). The walkers were literally stamping to death an area that was meant to be preserved so that they could enjoy its natural beauty.

The response of the Park authority was to appoint a project officer, nine field assistants and even a graphic designer (plenty of job-creation there) and to hire a helicopter from the Royal Air Force to fly in tons of aggregate so that new paths could be laid. So much for the 'traditional' landscape. The authority also felt it necessary to apologize for 'any inconvenience caused to walkers', the very people who had done the damage in the first place. 'Few can deny that the project is necessary and the money well spent,' the authority added. The disinterested observer, however, might well question the thinking that led to the necessity of the project and wonder about the wisdom of spending half a million pounds so that it can all happen again. 'The choice had to be made between restoration work, letting the footpaths become mudbaths, or keeping people off the hills to allow the paths to recover on their own,' said the Three Peaks project officer, Simon Rose. 'Restoration was the only acceptable option.' Why, in the name of sanity? And acceptable to whom? Our disinterested observer might be inclined to think that the only acceptable course would have been either to stop the marching feet for a time – a perfectly justifiable course since they actually caused the damage – or to have found a way of making the quarter of a million walkers pay for their depredations.

Instead, the Park authority, in the 1987 edition of its newsletter (significantly entitled *The Visitor*), encouraged still more people to go to the Park, boasting that at a cost of only fourteen pence a head National Parks were 'good value for money' and showing a photograph of a happy couple with boots and rucksacks doing precisely the sort of thing that had led to a bill of £500,000. It did not appear to think it odd that, a few pages later, it was bemoaning 'the devastation caused by walkers in the Three Peaks'. Clearly, Park authorities see the solution to their conflicting responsibilities as the provision of more money by the government so that they can carry out more restoration work in more areas damaged by more visitors. That view may have its attractions; what it lacks is any sort of logic.

The Parks do have a case for saying that they are seriously underfinanced. After the announcement of the 1988–9 budget allocations, one county councillor described the 'self-congratulatory attitude' of the Countryside Commission as 'nauseating', adding that the Commission 'lacks intelligence and is capable of considerable self-delusion'. One is driven to wonder, however, about the degree of delusion among the Park authorities themselves and about the way they spend the money they do have. Still in the Dales, while the Park committee complained loudly about its shortage of funds and cut its spending by 5 per cent, it nevertheless decided in 1988 to add to its burdens by committing itself to saving derelict barns and crumbling stone walls for posterity. 'Unless we can find an acceptable solution and make significant progress within the next five to ten years, this distinctive landscape may have gone beyond the point of no return,' said the Park officer in that tone of hectoring urgency beloved of conservationists. 'At present there is little economic justification for owners to keep redundant barns and walls in good repair. We hope that, if we can provide most of the finance, we might encourage farmers to keep them intact.'

Here is Robert Hewison's heritage industry in action in the countryside. It is admitted that the barns are no use to anybody and the walls are not needed, but they have suddenly become national assets, an essential part of 'tradition' and we must preserve them (by, in effect, buying them, of course) for posterity. Not only that, but we have in a sense already been paying for the destruction of these treasures, because the policy of the publicly financed National Park has been to demand that new buildings in its area be constructed of 'traditional' materials – not wattle and daub, fortunately, but stone and slate, the tradition that the conservationists have selected as the correct one. Naturally, the tradition in the building trade having changed somewhat during the past couple of centuries, it is not easy for builders in the Dales to obtain such things as stone roofing flags. There is, though, one abundant source: the old, unwanted, derelict barns that litter the fields and that nobody cared much about until the Park authority decided they must be restored, for no good reason other than that they are there. Of course, with the demand for housing in North Yorkshire and the popularity of barn conversions ... but at this point I dare not tread farther along such a heretical path. The Park officer's solution? 'I will be pleased to open discussions with anyone with the skills to reopen a small-scale mine or quarry and work stone for roofing.' It could almost be the motto of the heritage industry: yesterday's answer to today's question.

In some cases, National Parks seem to see their conservation policy as encompassing improvements on nature's work, rather in the manner of the formal landscape painters who portrayed trees in places other than where they actually occurred, so as to achieve a more pleasing composition. Early in 1988, the North York Moors authority pledged £30,000, and asked the government for more, to destroy up to 20,000 acres of bracken growing on moorland no longer used for grazing. While admitting that land not under 'management' might be good for wildlife in some instances, the Park officer felt that 'traditional' moorland was being lost to the encroaching bracken, though there might be a case for allowing some of it to survive at the edges of the moors. Heaven forbid that land should be allowed to revert to wilderness – we are talking about a park, after all. And while they are about it, the Park authorities would like to indulge in a little tree-planting and restoration of stone walls and provision of fencing, all in the name of 'traditional' moorland, of course.

If the attitude in National Park circles towards nature is ambiguous, so it is towards agriculture. While much energy, and money, is expended on trying to persuade farmers to use land less intensively, practical steps to achieve this aim are frequently greeted with dire warnings about the risks to the countryside. 'Better the devil you know,' seems to be the prevailing attitude. The government's announcement in 1988 that it intended to implement the European Community's extensification scheme to reduce beef and cereal surpluses brought complaints from Park officials that attempts to divert to alternative uses land now given over to grazing and cereal production might disrupt 'traditional' farming patterns and spoil the landscape. Yet is it not the same National Park authorities who constantly tell us that 'the traditional farming landscape' has been threatened since the war 'by intensification of farming methods', and is it not that very intensification that the government is seeking to stop? 'We are not opposed to change,' says the Countryside Commission. Indeed not, just so long as it does not actually change anything.

The question that arises from all this is what precisely our National Parks are for. The simple answer is that we do not really know. If their primary purpose was to preserve parts of the country considered to be outstandingly beautiful and culturally valuable, then why is it that many districts outside them have been designated Areas of Outstanding Natural Beauty, with different sets of rules? Surely such areas should be National Parks? Clearly the Parks are not intended to maintain wildernesses, like the American version, in which plants and animals can flourish more or less unchecked: there are no wildernesses to speak of in England, and the land which comes nearest to the wild state is largely the responsibility of the Nature Conservancy Council, though the National Trust is also involved, and in fact owns 2500 square miles within the ten National Parks. The Parks' justification of support for the local community is at best debatable; most often it takes the form of a sort of nannying role based on the apparent assumption that locals cannot be trusted to deal properly with their own countryside. In the Peak District, for example, the National Park authority felt it necessary to purchase 6400 acres of East Moor (with the help of a grant of £350,000 and a loan of £75,000 from the National Heritage Memorial Fund) and then to employ its own shepherd to 'manage' sheep grazed there by local farmers, the clear implication being that the farmers in question could not manage it themselves to the standards of the conservation ethic. Furthermore, though the Parks claim their planning policy is often more flexible than that of some local councils, the fact is that serious development in National Parks is generally discouraged by planning requirements, if not actually blocked, a situation that does little to help rural communities short of jobs, housing and services. The amount of employment the Parks themselves offer is minimal.

We are left, then, with 'public access for open-air recreation', but even here – as the Ramblers Association and others will testify – the position of the Parks is ambivalent, to say the least. The following extracts from an official guide to 'Your Rights in the Countryside' summarize the problems:

102

Am I allowed to walk where I like?
No ... In general, walkers must stick to public rights of way ...
In certain areas the national park authority has negotiated
public access agreements with the owner and you are free to
roam as you please ... However, there are restrictions on
access during grouse shooting and at times of high fire risk ...
In some places walkers have crossed private land for many
years through the goodwill of the owner although there is no
statutory right of access.

Surely I can wander at will over open moorland?
The public does not have a statutory right of access to open
moorland, apart from along rights of way, of course. In some
places extra paths have been used by walkers for many years
with no complaint from the landowner, but in others the
public is not welcome ... A lot of moorland is common land
but this does not give the public right of access at the moment.

Where can I camp or park my caravan?
Only where you have the permission of the landowner, even
on moorland.

In short, the right of public access in a National Park is very little
different from what it would be anywhere else, although it is true
that the agreements mentioned in answer to the first question can
and do offer visitors rather greater freedom to wander than might
otherwise be the case. The difficulties arising from the increasing
desire to use the countryside for leisure activities are discussed at
length in Chapter Six; but the Three Peaks disaster and other
evidence of the ravages of tourism, in the Lake District for example,
should call into question the policy of opening up the wilder parts
of Britain to please the huddled urban masses.

I have concentrated on the Parks because they present the most
obvious sign of the confusion that exists about how the more
beautiful parts of Britain should be regarded, what purpose they
might fulfil in a small country and how they should be treated.
However, the apparently unbridled passion for conservation has

also led to the spattering of the countryside with Areas of Outstanding Natural Beauty, Environmentally Sensitive Areas, Sites of Special Scientific Interest, Heritage Coasts, nature reserves, National Trust lands, national scenic areas in Scotland, bird sanctuaries and so on, not to mention legislation that protects particular species or prohibits the picking of wildflowers. Sometimes it seems that there is hardly an area of the country that is not subject to some regulation or other, which is not at all in keeping with the physical and spiritual freedom the countryside is supposed to symbolize. All this activity is, of course, supported by organizations, both official and ad hoc, which dedicate themselves either locally or nationally to overseeing and monitoring it or to campaigning for even more. The National Parks, for instance, have not only the Countryside Commission and local committees, but also the voluntary Council for National Parks and a campaign known as 'Watch over the National Parks'.

Then there are the Nature Conservancy Council, the Council for the Protection of Rural England, English Heritage, the National Heritage Memorial Fund, the National Trust, the British Trust for Conservation Volunteers, the Royal Society for the Protection of Birds, and countless local or specialized groups, all with a stake in the conservation and heritage industries. More than three million people in Britain now belong to one or more of the multiplicity of conservationist organizations. Inevitably, this abundance of interest, expertise and commitment leads at the very least to duplication of effort and also to the sort of competition for funds, both public and charitable, that results in available resources being spread too thinly, so that no organization receives quite enough money to do its job properly and the public becomes utterly confused as to who does what. In the end everyone, including the worthy groups themselves, is dissatisfied.

In common with many other aspects of British life that are now taken for granted, conservation has developed hugger-mugger, carried along by a sometimes unwarranted sense of urgency and crisis, devoid of real thought or planning, without any serious questioning of underlying assumptions, often heedless of consequences outside the narrow field of a particular enthusiasm. A lot of people said we should have national parks, and, lo, there were national parks, complete with an impressive set of contradictions so intractable that they ensure the ideals behind their creation can never be achieved. When it is realized that the parks do not fulfil what was hoped of them, we move into Areas of Outstanding Natural Beauty, and when they fall short of aspirations we create Environmentally Sensitive Areas. Everybody complains – we are doing either too much or too little – but the guiding principles are never challenged.

No sensible person can now doubt that there is a need for conservation in the real sense of the word. The assumption that our ancestors had more respect than we do for something called 'nature' (as if human beings were excluded) is only partly justified. History suggests that man alters his environment to the limits of his knowledge and technology, and there is no evidence that our forebears, given the practical restrictions, would have been any more careful than we have been in modern times. In spite of that, however, the pace of change in modern times and the pressures of a vastly larger population mean that we have a much more dramatic effect on our surroundings than our forebears did and we risk losing much more that may be valuable. What we have to deter-mine is what we wish to conserve, how we should go about it, and what conservation is meant to achieve. The Countryside Review Committee, in the discussion paper of 1978 I quoted at the beginning of this chapter, spoke of a squandering of resources, but what it meant appears never to have been fully understood. Conservationists often refer to the countryside as 'a resource', implying that it falls into one simple category. This is not the case. The countryside is not one resource, but a whole series of resources, and in order to distinguish between them we must, in effect, start again from the beginning, recognizing the diversity of our rural assets.

The National Parks should become precisely what their present misnomer implies, instead of trying to carry out some of the functions of the American original in a country where the pattern of land distribution is both entirely different and longer estab-lished. They should be sited on land that is publicly owned –

bought if necessary – and dedicated to the nation to use as it will, for sport and leisure, camping, caravanning or simply wandering about. They should include woodlands, lakes, rivers, meadows, mountains and moorlands, but in smaller quantities scattered throughout the country, not as at present concentrated in economically deprived areas of England and Wales (there are no National Parks in the prosperous South-East). For preference, they should not include farms, villages and towns, for while they do the conflict between national benefit and local interest can never be satisfactorily resolved. They must be supervised by a national parks authority whose responsibility it would be to maintain them in a fit and proper state for the various public uses to which they would be put, and they must be properly financed and staffed through a combination of taxes, as a national asset open to all, and fees, possibly in the form of an additional subscription system for people most likely to take advantage of them.

The conservationist role must be a completely separate one, and could be undertaken in a variety of ways. The first requirement is to identify accurately the ecological, environmental and cultural values we wish to preserve and our purpose in so doing. If the most important aim is to protect wildlife, then the area should become a national nature reserve (as some already are) and the land should be taken into ownership and management by, say, the Nature Conservancy Council or the National Trust, depending perhaps upon whether the degree of protection was to be on scientific grounds or whether limited numbers of the public (bird-watchers, amateur botanists, school parties and so forth) were to be admitted at the discretion of the managing authority. Other organizations, such as the Royal Society for the Protection of Birds or even local groups with the ability and support to raise money for land purchase, could be encouraged to operate in a similar way, though not with Treasury finance. The imposition of a small tax levy for ecological purposes would, over time, lead to general awareness and acceptance of both collective and personal responsibility for maintaining wildlife in these islands, while those with a special interest in the natural world would be free to make whatever contribution they thought appropriate as well. Again, though, such nature reserves should be kept as small as possible, taking account of the space required for them to be effective and the economic needs of the local community. There is no reason why rural development and wildlife protection cannot co-exist sensibly, provided the demands of both are thoroughly examined and understood.

The sort of nature reserves I have described would no doubt include Sites of Special Scientific Interest, which are already protected under the Wildlife and Countryside Acts, but some care would have to be taken with regard to the newly created Environmentally Sensitive Areas, of which there were nineteen in 1988, many in marginal farming country though including the Somerset Levels and the South Downs. As I indicated in Chapter Two, the purpose of these areas is not entirely clear and may be less altruistic than the Ministry of Agriculture would have us believe. Some farmers have welcomed them, though, seeing the grants as a way of improving their incomes, and so long as the scheme remains entirely voluntary there is no real harm in it. A reduction in the number of agricultural enterprises in marginal areas, which I have suggested may be inevitable, could be exploited to return some of these areas to a genuinely wild state, while others might be operated as 'model' farms to appease those whose desire seems to be to see the countryside return to what it was half a century ago. On the other hand, scientific developments in agriculture may in time allow such areas to be worked profitably and without harm to the environment, so it would be sensible not to permit the ESA concept to spread too wide or to become an institution.

Conservation in a wider sense, of landscape and rural life, is a much trickier problem demanding reliance on fewer assumptions and more careful thought. The kind of conflicts that can arise is well illustrated by the case of one of the most recent designations of an Area of Outstanding Natural Beauty, that affecting the North Pennines in County Durham in 1986. The initiative came from the Countryside Commission, which sought the government's approval for the AONB designation of 860 square miles, the largest such area in the country and bigger than any National Park except the Lake District. The proposal was supported by Durham County Council but opposed by the district councils in Teesdale and Weardale, at least fourteen parish councils and the National Farmers Union, all of whom shared the fear of large numbers of residents that much-needed development and employment prospects would be stifled by what they saw as the imposition of beauty-spot status. Such was the scale of the opposition that a public inquiry was ordered. After five weeks of evidence and ten months of deliberation, the government inspector, Sir Stephen Berthon, decided that 85 per cent of the proposed area should become an AONB, but the main population centres of Teesdale and Weardale – towns such as Barnard Castle and Witton-le-Wear, along with their surrounding villages – should be excluded, on the ground that their scenery did not meet the required criteria. Even-handedly he also left out Hamsterley Forest which, though considered attractive by many people, borders an area of somewhat run-down former mining villages.

Sir Stephen commented that he did not believe the designation would adversely affect industry in the area, except where it would be thought necessary to preserve the quality of the landscape. That, of course, was the point. There is a large cement works at Eastgate in the Wear Valley (part of the strip left out of the AONB for obvious reasons), and the district as a whole is particularly suitable for mining and quarrying, in which it saw at least some opportunities for future development. As an Area of Outstanding Natural Beauty, it must now accept that new large industrial or commercial developments will be regarded as 'inconsistent', except where they can be shown to be in the national interest and when no alternative site is available. Applications for new or extended mineral workings will be subject to rigorous examination, with in practice the balance of probabilities against them.

The 'battle of the North Pennines' was widely regarded as a victory among conservationists, though many of them still complained about the 'second-class' status of AONB designation: they wanted another National Park. Grants of more than £500,000 over five years were not enough, they said; there was no power to prevent 'destructive' farming practices or afforestation, no right of public access to private land, no planning mechanism automatically to prevent further mining and quarrying. Rather a hollow victory, then, one might think. Certainly the people of the area could be forgiven for thinking so. The Durham Dales cover almost 42 per cent of the county but support only 2.5 per cent of its population. During the past twenty-five years more than a quarter of the people who used to live in the Dales have left, and since 1972 the total number of jobs in the area has declined by almost a third. By 1996, unless something is done to reverse the trend, a further 2000 people are expected to have left the Dales, and the unemployment rate among those who remain is likely to be about 25 per cent. The Countryside Commission claimed rather smugly that, as an AONB, 'the North Pennines can enjoy the benefits of both conservation and support for the local economy'. In fact, as a direct result of the new status, about fifteen new jobs were to be provided in the area over the following ten years: not much support there for the local economy. But, it is argued, official recognition of the region's beauty will attract tourists. The signs are not encouraging. The Durham Dales now receive only about one and a quarter million visitors a year, a fraction of the numbers flocking to, say, the Lake District or the Yorkshire Dales, and most go only for the day. It may be some time before the people of the North Pennines Area of Outstanding Natural Beauty feel the benefits of the honour bestowed upon them.

The whole concept of the blanket 'protection' of landscape is highly questionable. The alert reader will have noticed that much of this chapter has been concerned with the north of England, and there is a reason for that. The counties that comprise the North in official terms – Cumbria, Northumberland and Durham – have among them some 29 per cent of their area given over to National Parks, as against only 10 per cent in England and Wales as a whole. In June 1987, a year after the designation of the new AONB in the North Pennines, the region had an unemployment rate of 15 per cent, second only to that of Northern Ireland, and the second highest (after Wales) number of 'economically inactive males', 41 per cent. The average household expenditure in the North was the lowest in Britain, at £145 a week. The inference was obvious: what the North needed was industry and commerce, development. What it had just received was 'protection' from development, at least in its countryside. In theory this may be all very well, for the countryside *is* some of the most beautiful in the land, but unless there is a change of 'conservation' policy it will also become some of the emptiest and poorest, condemned by its natural beauty to a lower standard of living than anywhere else.

By 1989 there had been some apparent improvement in the unemployment position of the North, with the average rate for the region down to 10.6 per cent of the work-force. How much this reduction had been achieved by means other than the provision of actual new permanent jobs – by, for example, changes to the counting system, the introduction of compulsory training schemes and the willingness of unemployed people to take part-time work – was a matter for debate, but in any case by far the largest number of employment opportunities that did appear were in urban areas. In February 1989, the predominantly rural county of Northumberland had an unemployment rate of 11.8 per cent, while in Durham county the rate was 12.1 per cent, calculated as a proportion of the sum of employees in employment and those without jobs, rather than on the number of benefit claimants. In the less well 'protected' South-East, by contrast, the rates calculated on the same basis, and excluding London, ranged from just 2.6 per cent in Berkshire to 5.5 per cent in East Sussex.

'What we find so attractive today', says one of the National Park newsletters, 'is the result of a joint effort between man and nature.' Yet the fundamental policy of conservationism as it is now practised appears to be to prevent man from carrying on his efforts. Who is to say that what we find so attractive today will be equally appreciated by our descendants in a couple of hundred years' time? Change, decay and regeneration are part of the natural cycle. Our countryside has changed many times and in many ways over the centuries, just as towns, cities and villages have been rebuilt many times. There are always things which survive, and no doubt there are those in need of protection so that they will survive, but it is the height of arrogance to fix upon our landscape *as it is now* and decree that it must always remain like that. The warning of the Countryside Review Committee about conservation as merely maintenance of the status quo seems to have been ignored.

I said that the countryside was not one resource but many. It is also a living organism in which people have an important part to play. Ignoring the human factor and treating the countryside like some sort of museum is likely to prove the best way of ensuring that it does not survive.

By all means let us protect parts of our 'rural heritage', if that is how we wish to view it, but we must keep a sense of proportion. There is no need for 800 square miles of County Durham to be placed, in effect, in a preserving jar. Eighty square miles might well suffice. The rest, left to itself, might 'suffer' from some development, but the chances are there would still be plenty of land that nobody wanted to develop. We must rid ourselves of the spurious sense of panic fostered by those who claim the countryside is disappearing about us or that, if we do not act now, it will be covered by concrete or conifers.

We should also resist the insidious idea that construction and the countryside do not go together. I have travelled on six-lane highways through some of the most breathtaking scenery in North America, over bridges and vast intersections that in no way detract from the beauty and grandeur of the surroundings. Closer to home, I would argue, for example, that the northern section of the M6 motorway cannot be said to 'spoil' the parts of Cumbria through which it passes, while the magnificent sweep of the Severn Bridge affords a unique view of the estuary. As for buildings, subject to certain minimal planning requirements, they can often add interest to a landscape that would otherwise have no more vitality than a picture postcard. If defunct barns are considered an essential part of the rural scene, why should houses not have equal value? Is it merely that the current 'conservation ethic' requires landscapes without figures?

The conservation movement has had its part to play in raising our level of awareness with regard to the value of our surroundings, but at the same time its essentially backward-looking attitude serves to obscure present and future possibilities. At the University of Wisconsin in the United States there are more than a hundred acres of thriving, traditional prairie – all of them man-made. The grasses, flowers and trees, more than two hundred species of them altogether, were collected from unused land in various parts of the state, replanted and carefully nurtured in a scientific recreation of their wild habitat, so that the wilderness was recreated more or less exactly as nature intended. The project was started forty years ago by an ecological visionary named Henry Greene, and since then the idea has steadily grown among imaginative environmentalists that man has not only the obligation but also the ability to make good what he has damaged in the name of progress.

Using similar methods, wetlands are now being revived (rebuilt, one might almost say) at a number of places in America and even more ambitious schemes have begun to replace lost redwood forests in California. The Bosques Colon project in the West Indies is creating new tropical forests and a parallel operation is under way with dry-forest in Costa Rica. In Britain, plant life displaced by the construction of the Channel Tunnel has been carefully preserved so that it can be recreated elsewhere – woodlands, for example, have been re-sited and the chalk waste from the digging is being desalinated and used to provide new habitats for downland flora. The more we learn about the biosphere, the more can be attempted; and such undertakings demonstrate that conservation in its most creative sense does not simply cling to the past, but places it in the context of the future.

Of course, there are some who object, saying that such copying of nature produces only fakes, yet it is obvious that rude nature itself relies on copying to reproduce itself. Virgin landscapes, such as dry riverbeds or lava fields, are populated by copies of plant species thriving elsewhere, often as a result of intervention by birds or insects. What is unnatural about human beings playing their part as nature's agents, too? Moreover, nature is the original genetic engineer, introducing 'errors' in its copying methods to adapt or improve species to allow them to survive in a changed environment. Are the results of such techniques any less 'real' when they are produced on the basis of human analysis? The point is that old cultural baggage needs to be discarded in the light of increasing knowledge and our approach to the natural world must become more flexible.

Frederick J. Turner, an American poet and academic much

interested in ecology, has argued cogently for both a more secular view of nature and a revised environmental – not simply conservation – ethic. We can, Turner wrote recently, 'glimpse the notion, fundamentally theological, that the world is a creation, and inferior to its creator. And underlying this notion there is, perhaps, that basic Indo-European habit of thought – a *human* habit of thought – that derives the nature of the child from the nature of the parents, and thus insists on the inferiority and subordination of child to parent.' Science, however, is broadening the horizons of understanding and we are beginning dimly to perceive that 'the branching tree of evolution brings about wonderfully new forms of life, unpredictable from their origins, or "predictable" only after they have appeared'. Thus our concept of what is 'natural' is gradually changing, and with it, surely, must change our view of mankind's role in the evolutionary process. We have not been slow to exploit medical advances that prolong life, not only by artificial means but also by re-using human material, and even techniques that create life in a test-tube. Are babies whose genetic material is assembled in a laboratory to be considered 'fake' human beings?

For preservationists of what Turner calls 'the old fire-and-brimstone school' the discipline of ecology is, he says, fundamentally elegiac, 'essentially a eulogy to what we humans have destroyed; their science is a postmortem, their myth is of a primal crime by which we are all tainted: the murder of nature'. Their study of nature is passive and classificatory, not concerned with action and experiment. 'It is possible to sympathise with such purists; they often serve as a conscience to humankind,' Turner adds. 'But human beings are just as often ill-served by them – people are not at their best when motivated by guilt or alarm. If not actually paralysed, they act mulishly, dutifully, without the joy and playfulness that liberate the imagination and start the flow of creative thought.'

Frederick Turner foresees a day when biological restoration becomes the norm in environmental terms. If he is right, then perhaps when we listen to all the clamour to preserve what we have in its existing condition we should bear in mind that conservation as we now understand it is quite likely to prove to be nothing more than a passing phase in the long history of the countryside. As always, the future will demand something different from what was demanded in the past.

FIVE

Problems of Development

The land of Britain is one of the most densely populated
areas in the world, and it is therefore of vital importance
in the public interest that competing claims to its use
should be settled in such a way that the necessary balance
between them is maintained.

Britain, An Official Handbook, 1953

The people who live in the rural areas of the northern part of England, of the West Country, of Scotland and of Wales enjoy some of the finest scenery these islands have to offer, and because of that, as I suggested in the last chapter, they tend to suffer from what might be called conservation blight. Such is the pressure to preserve our wildest landscapes – all of them – that serious industrial development which would help to improve economic conditions in the rural parts of those regions simply cannot take place.

There are, of course, various efforts, with both public and private finance, to revitalize the run-down urban areas such as Teesside, Liverpool, Glasgow, Cardiff, Newport and Swansea, but in development terms, the distinction between town and country appears to be absolute. Recent research suggests that in Britain as a whole, something like a quarter of rural households are suffering economic deprivation – in layman's terms, they are poor – and official figures indicate that the national average is exceeded in the areas I have mentioned. (Northern Ireland helps to increase the figure, too, but that has special development problems which have little to do with the beauty of its landscape.) Rural poverty, however, is largely ignored, because its surroundings are so very much prettier than the urban variety. Jobs in the countryside, it seems, must take second place to the view.

In the prosperous south-eastern corner of England, by contrast, the perception in many rural areas is of hordes of greedy developers massing for an invasion, intent on extending urban sprawl as far as the eye can see. Indeed, delegates to the Conservative Party Conference in Brighton in 1988 were picketed by protesters chanting, 'Leave our green fields!' Another manifestation, perhaps, of the much quoted North–South Divide, which is, to express it more accurately, really a divergence of needs and desires between the South-East and the rest of the country. In both cases, however, the effect of the situation is the same: a degree of protectionism that inhibits development outside urban areas and, many people argue, seriously hampers efforts to modernize the nation and improve its economic performance.

The government, mainly in an attempt to reduce agricultural production, as I have explained, announced in 1987 a programme of what it called rural enterprise and development. In an official booklet, the Department of the Environment recognized that great changes were taking place in rural life and that the process was likely to continue:

While agriculture remains the dominant form of land use in rural areas, it employed some 500,000 people in England and Wales in 1986 or just under 2.5 per cent of the working population. The Population Census for 1981 showed that even in predominantly rural areas, where just 4.9 million or 10 per cent of the population lived in 1981, the percentage working in agriculture was 14 per cent compared with 58 per cent in services, transport etc. and 28 per cent in manufacturing and construction. These figures show that the rural areas as a whole are increasing in population and, since employment in agriculture has been falling for many years, the majority of those who live in the rural areas are engaged in other types of employment ... In fact there is now a growing diversity of employment and economic activity in rural Britain. New types of industry, including those based on new technologies, are locating in country towns, and new small firms, whether specialising in computer services or traditional crafts, are setting up in rural areas.

This optimistic assessment, however, must be viewed in the light of one or two other facts. First, the government's booklet admits: 'The transfer of agricultural land to urban uses has been declining sharply compared to the rates seen in the 1950s and 1960s when some 15,000 hectares of farmland each year was taken for development. Between 1980 and 1985 the figure was less than 5000 hectares per annum.' That rate of transfer is lower than at any time since the 1920s, which tends to suggest that most of what is called rural development is taking place not in the countryside but, as stated in the previous paragraph, in towns. Second, figures compiled for the Department of the Environment by Ordnance Survey show that 'nearly half of all new housing in England in 1985 was built on derelict or redeveloped sites or unused land in urban areas'. Not much sign there of a serious effort to modernize the countryside. Third, and perhaps most telling, there is the government's own statement of its objectives, which are 'the renewal of our older towns and cities; the protection of the countryside; and the preservation of the Green Belts'. This, it must be emphasized, is a booklet dedicated to rural enterprise and development, yet what the rural areas are actually offered is protection of the countryside and preservation of the Green Belts.

The House Builders Federation, in its evidence to the Duke of Edinburgh's controversial Inquiry into British Housing in 1985, stated:

The problem facing house-purchasers is that artificially created land shortages push the price of homes beyond their pockets, while housebuilders are increasingly being forced to ignore significant sections of the market ... If we fail to explode the myths on which so many of our housing and planning policies are based, Britain will once again face a major housing crisis by the end of the decade. Moreover, that crisis will directly and adversely affect economic recovery and growth, because limitations on the supply of land affect both levels of employment and industrial activity.

The Federation supported its claim of an artificially created land shortage with a nationwide survey of planning policies. In the North-West, it found that such policies had actually reduced housing opportunities in north Cheshire and the south of Greater Manchester, even though these were areas of high demand. The general strategy in the region was to 'direct growth back to urban areas', notwithstanding the problems of poor environment and limited availability of jobs in many towns. From Wales, the Federation reported that local authorities were imposing restrictive planning policies in spite of government estimates that 11,000 new houses would be needed in the principality each year. The West Glamorgan authority, having allocated land for housing in West Swansea, later refused planning permission for the land, while in Gwent planning permission referred to 'areas that have in the past been less attractive to home buyers'. In Newport, where demand was highest, development opportunities were restricted to just two locations, both of which were likely to be expensive for building. 'The effect will be to restrict the choice of location for home buyers and will result in an acute short-fall of new homes throughout the county.'

In the Midlands, the Federation forecast that demand in War-wickshire, Shropshire and Staffordshire would be significantly higher than the number of new houses allowed for by local councils. Warwickshire, for example, was 'refusing to acknowledge the pressures of demand for housing and employment which are already building up in anticipation of the completion of the M40 and M42 motorways'. The situation was similar in the East Midlands, with Derbyshire concentrating on the establishment of the Green Belt and Leicestershire looking at only one area for its housing provision.

One of the regions where the demand for housing is highest is the South-West, which during the past few years has consistently recorded the highest level of inward migration in Britain, the annual figure doubling to 46,000 between 1984 and 1986. Here the House Builders Federation found that the county structure plan for Somerset sought to maintain housing provision at some 38 per cent below past rates; building in Gloucestershire was to drop from an annual average of 2600 to 2100; Devon was offering land for building in areas of low demand, such as Honiton, while resisting development round Exeter, where many people were seeking houses. A similar situation existed in East Anglia, which in 1986 became the fastest growing region of Britain with a population increase over the previous five years of 5.1 per cent and 13 per cent growth estimated by the year 2001. Cambridge was accused of preparing to create a short-fall of 200 acres of industrial land and a serious lack of housing by adopting a strict Green Belt policy, though on my own evidence development seemed to be proceeding apace round Peterborough to the north. In more rural parts of the region, planning policy appeared to insist that new housing be confined mostly to existing settlements, with the result that vacant sites in small villages were filled with often inappropriate buildings, sometimes very tightly packed, and local traffic congestion was increased quite dramatically.

In the South-East the situation has become quite tense, as the demonstrations at the Conservative conference proved. Greater London and the Home Counties contain 30 per cent of the population of Britain, living in a density varying from 220 people per square kilometre to 4291. Although in 1986 the population of Greater London stabilized, after declining for twenty-five years, it still showed a net migration of 49,000 people, many of whom moved into rural areas within easy commuting distance of the city. In Buckinghamshire, for example, the population rose by more than 7 per cent. Yet the House Builders Federation had found that 'all shire counties are seeking to restrict growth opportunities, notably by cutting back on the levels of housing provision in structure plans'. Some aspects of such a policy were hard to understand: Hertfordshire was discovered to be promoting jobs and office growth but at the same time reducing levels of house-building by 17 per cent. The south-eastern counties, the Federation concluded, were planning to keep out the people who wished to move from London.

Further north the situation was quite different and the pressures were other than demographic, except in places such as County Durham, where planning policy had been designed (with little success, it now seems) to prevent further decline in areas devastated by the loss of mining and heavy industry. In the North-East in general, according to the Federation, policies were 'restraining new developments in attractive locations in favour of directing development to declining areas such as some inner urban areas of Tyneside where demand for new housing is relatively low' – though people who could afford rapidly rising house prices were still moving to the countryside in order to escape high urban domestic rates, thereby contributing to inner-city decline. In Yorkshire and Humberside there was a lack of housing sites and local authorities were restricting further releases, so house prices would soar, the Federation said. It was right, with Dales cottages doubling in value in a little more than two years. Prices were also unexpectedly high in Scotland, which still records a level of home ownership among the lowest in Europe, because of protectionist policies towards land. Even round Glasgow, the scene of an ambitious regeneration programme, not enough building land was being released to maintain the momentum, while the 'blanket Green Belt policy' in Edinburgh meant that many buyers were having to settle for flats in the city.

Of course it may be said that the House Builders Federation has an axe to grind: its members, after all, are in the business of building new houses. Moreover, there have been some changes in the situation since its report was compiled, caused partly by further increases in industrial activity and partly by soaring property prices, a trend that began in London, peaking in 1988, and later spread throughout the country, where by 1989 the best that could be said was that the market had stabilized. None the less, the changes that have occurred have, as I pointed out in Chapter Three, led to increased demand for rural housing without a corresponding rise in availability, and the main argument of the Federation is supported by official statistics.

The builders' case is that there is in Britain no shortage of land for housing. That would seem to be borne out by the conversion rates for agricultural land admitted by the Department of the Environment. The problem is that rigidly applied and, it may be thought, outdated planning controls, together with ever-widening powers of 'protecting' the landscape, have combined to limit artificially the amount of land available for building, thus reducing housing starts to a level well below demand and forcing up prices beyond the reach of many people wishing to move to better or new homes. Twenty years ago, the Federation argues, the price of land represented just 10–15 per cent of the price of a new house; in the 1980s that proportion has risen in some areas to between 30 and 40 per cent.

Let us consider the figures, provided by the Central Statistical Office in 1988. In the South-East, the *average* proportion of land cost in the price of a new house, outside Greater London, was indeed 39 per cent. The *average* weighted price of building land had almost trebled, from an index of 100 in the base year of 1980 to one of 297 six years later. Throughout the country, less dramatic but equally significant rises suggest a general lack of new building land, though differences in the types of site and the sort of housing provided make land/price proportions difficult to compare.

If there is a shortage of land available for new housing, does it really matter? The House Builders Federation says it does: though the rate of population growth has declined in recent years, with the increase by the end of the century estimated at about two million, social and demographic changes mean that the number of *households* is rising rapidly. A growing proportion of single and divorced people and an ageing population that generally lives longer all affect housing demand, and the forecast is that by 1991 nearly a million new households will have been formed in Great Britain: that equates almost exactly with the total number of new houses currently being built each year, allowing little leeway for the replacement of obsolescent housing (almost a third of all the houses in Britain were built before 1914, and in some parts of the country the figure approaches a half). In fact, the overall housing stock has been increasing on average by only 1 per cent a year for the past ten years and new houses are currently being built at an annual rate of only three per thousand of the population. What all these rather indigestible figures mean is that we are, in effect, standing still.

In 1988, the number of new housing starts reached 220,000, but in 1989 the annual figure was expected to drop back to only a little above the 1984 total of 160,000. At the same time, a report by British architects revealed that there were throughout the country a million houses that could be officially classified as unfit for human habitation. Even if, as some experts suggested in 1989, the rate of creation of new households was slowing, there must be added to that number a substantial group of people whose living conditions are not those of the late twentieth century and who ought to be rehoused.

As Secretary of State for the Environment, Nicholas Ridley joined the House Builders Federation in suggesting that more land should be released for more houses, though his attention was concentrated mainly on the South-East, where more than 600,000 new dwellings were needed according to the estimates of his department in 1988. This need was disputed by a former Environment Secretary, Michael Heseltine, who appeared to have come down on the side of the 'Leave our green fields!' lobby. Heseltine, whose parliamentary constituency in Oxfordshire was 'threatened' in 1988 by plans for an ambitious development including 6000 new houses on what was then 1200 acres of open fields, spoke out in favour of direction of population movement away from the South-East. 'Should you not look at the composition of the population movement,' he asked after the Brighton conference, 'to see if there's anything government can do? The moment you ask that question you discover the fascinating situation that a quarter of a million people every year leave the South-East, voluntarily, to retire, to move to more distant parts of Great Britain. But what is happening as a quarter of a million people go is that another quarter of a million people come to take their place, from areas, largely, of high or higher unemployment.' Those newcomers, he added, should be encouraged to stay where they are by being provided with jobs and being offered better housing.

That might well be a solution for the South-East, the Conservative Party heartland, where many traditional Tory voters were appalled at the prospect of their comfortable, quasi-rural lives being disrupted by the very free-market policies they had supported for ten years. It would do little to help the rest of the country, many parts of which are already suffering, in the form of housing shortages and prices higher than locals can afford, as a result of Heseltine's quarter of a million refugees a year from the South-East. In a report entitled *The Future for Rural Communities*, published in 1988, the Association of District Councils said that all rural areas were experiencing housing difficulties, their stocks thrown out of balance by an inflow of people who wanted to combine country life with continued employment in urban areas and by those able to afford second or retirement homes. The chairman of the Association's rural needs panel, Nicholas Wilson, commented: 'The recent surge in property prices is denying private housing to local people who cannot afford as much as newcomers. This particularly hits younger people looking for first homes.'

The district councils see part of the answer as shared-equity schemes operated by housing associations, where buyers do not own their properties outright and must sell them back to the association if they move. Such arrangements may compensate for the recent sharp decline in the provision of public housing, but they would surely reduce many country people to the position of second-class citizens at a time when owner-occupation in Britain as a whole has reached 63 per cent and surveys have shown that 80 per cent of the adult population see owning their own houses as their ultimate aim. There is a much simpler and more effective option: if we do not need as much land as we have for farming – and clearly we do not – then more of it must be released for domestic and industrial building.

A general reluctance to face up to the need for development in rural areas, even to resist it, arises from much the same source as the years of refusal to recognize that agricultural policy was long overdue for radical change. This is that assumptions and forecasts made forty years ago, and strategies based on them, have taken on the inviolability of gospel, with the result that any attempt to challenge them appears heretical. To state it frankly, our planning regulations, and the requirements on which they were based, are wildly out of date. A balance is not being maintained between competing claims for land use and neither are such claims being settled in the public interest, especially that part of the public that lives in rural areas.

The concept of town and country planning as we now understand it was established as long ago as 1909, but in those happy days it was not considered proper for governments to interfere too much or too directly in the lives of their citizens and the powers given to local authorities were limited enough not to restrict developers in any serious way. The building boom of the years between the two world wars, which produced extensive suburbanization, resulted in greater efforts to control development, but it was not until 1945 that the first outlines of what remains at bottom our planning policy today appeared on the statute book. That venerable institution the Town and Country Planning Act became law in 1947 and, according to the present Department of the Environment, while there have been changes and improvements in the detailed procedures laid down by the Act, 'it remains probably the most comprehensive and effective land-use system in the world'. As recently as 1985 the government was boasting of how well that system had served the country and denying scurrilous rumours that it was about to be scrapped.

One of the effects of the Town and Country Planning Act 1947 was the establishment of Green Belts round cities and towns, stretches of land on which building would be permanently and severely restricted. This was not a new idea, since it dated from feudal times, when the purposes of empty patches of land included growing food for townspeople, acting as a barrier against the spread of disease and making it more difficult for an enemy to attack the town. None of those requirements carries much weight today, of course, so the planners sought other means of justification, as the Environment Department explains: 'Some towns are already too big for the comfort or the pleasure of the citizens, while others tend to merge with one another and need to be prevented from doing so. Many towns have expanded rapidly during the last hundred years and particularly since the advent of motor traffic. Some have coalesced with others to form huge conurbations where building seems endless and the boundary between different communities has become no more than a line on a map. Main roads have been lined with houses on both sides, to the detriment of traffic, and the distinction between town and country has become blurred.'

Every one of those statements is patently open to challenge. When, for example, does a town become too big for the comfort or pleasure of its citizens, and why must towns be prevented from merging with one another? The advent of motor traffic might have caused urban expansion, but it has also allowed easier access to the countryside – or at least it would have if a serious road building programme had been undertaken to keep pace with the growth of traffic. Among the reasons why Britain is so lacking in good roads are the Green Belt strategy and the general inadequacy of planning policy, which makes it nonsensical for the Environment Department to argue that main roads have become congested because they have houses on either side. It is also difficult to understand why different communities need visible boundaries between them (unless they are considering declaring themselves independent) and just how, in a country whose land area is distributed 80 per cent in favour of agriculture, there can be much confusion between town and country.

The real reason for the Green Belt is to be found in what the Department casually calls its secondary purpose: 'It is to provide opportunity to escape from the noise, congestion and strain of city life and to seek recreation in the countryside. Sometimes people may want to take part in organized games or sports or to pursue some scientific or artistic study or interest. More often they are content just to ramble or ride with no other object than to enjoy the scenery, fresh air and sunshine.' Here, enshrined in law, is the great rural myth with which I began this salutary journey through the British countryside. As the perceptive and witty journalist Stephen Pile summarized it:

What this love of the countryside is really all about is our refusal or inability to cope with cities. We have no concept of urbanity. The idea that it is possible to lead a pleasant and civilized life in the city is one that would never occur to a Briton. (No Italian would ever leave Rome or Florence to live in the dark and barbarous countryside to which even the farmers commute.)

... It is based upon the notion that the city is a bad place full of unhappy people, while the countryside is a good place, packed with happy, honest, decent folk.

This rural dream would be harmless enough, just another quaint British eccentricity, were it not for the fact that it has come to rule our lives, impede our progress and blind us to reality. Not only that, but our collective refusal to see the countryside as it is, and even to consider that it might have a future different from the idealized past with which we have endowed it, is actually helping to realize the urban nightmare that seems to haunt us. Far from making towns and cities more pleasant places to live in, the effect of the Green Belt mentality – and its extension into National Parks, Areas of Outstanding Natural Beauty and all the paraphernalia of rampant, unthinking conservation – is to increase the 'noise, congestion and strain' of urban existence. In 1984 the government added another element to Green Belt policy, stating: 'The aim is that by firmly maintaining the Green Belts, and preventing outward expansion, developers and others will be encouraged to turn their attention to opportunities for renewal and redevelopment within the urban areas.' What this means – quite apart from the fact that, according to the House Builders Federation, there is not enough land within urban areas to satisfy the demand for development – is that instead of expanding, the towns and cities become more dense as houses, shops, offices and factories fill in any open spaces that remain. The resulting sense of overcrowding in turn increases the desire of city-dwellers to move to the countryside, but since significant development is not permitted in rural areas, they must commute back to the urban areas to earn their living. This does not help the towns because commuting increases traffic congestion and it does not help rural areas because, in becoming dormitories for urban workers, their economy is distorted: house prices rise sharply, for instance, so that local young people, even if they might find employment in their area, are forced to move to towns anyway in order to secure somewhere to live that they can afford.

To be fair, the Conservative government that took office in 1979 became increasingly aware that changes were necessary in planning regulations, but in spite of successive election victories it appeared not to dare to adopt the same radical approach towards development in the countryside that had characterized its policies on nationalized industries, the welfare system and education, among other things. Kenneth Baker, when he was Secretary of State for the Environment, outlined the problem to the house-building industry late in 1985:

You, like us, have been pressing for due account to be taken of market demand. It is your customers, individual house buyers, who want homes in attractive parts of the country. If the great majority of house buyers wanted to live in the inner cities, you would need no bidding from me to go and build there.

But I have to tell you an unpalatable truth: you are still not winning friends. However unjustly, new housebuilding is too often seen as a blot on the landscape, as the despoiling of the countryside in pursuit of profit. As I go round the country – and particularly the South East – I am told repeatedly that people have had enough of development, and want us to call a halt to it. This point of view is becoming more and more insistent.

Neither local government nor central government can ignore the groundswell of opinion against the scale of development of the recent past. It is no consolation to be told that development is taking only a fraction of a per cent of our countryside, if that fraction includes your favourite view.

This, in its crudest terms, is the Nimby syndrome – Not In My Back Yard. The fact is that in the South-East region, excluding London, only 12.6 per cent of the total land area is urban; 42 per cent is designated Green Belt or Area of Outstanding Natural Beauty. Yet every time an important building project is suggested, every time a new trunk road or even a by-pass is planned, almost every time planning permission is even hinted at for redundant farmland, there is an outcry that the countryside is being raped and pillaged. Of course, development and modernization are necessary, just so long as they take place somewhere else. The objectives of Green Belt and countryside policy, worthy enough in their time and no doubt necessary in view of the careless and often ugly developments of earlier generations, have been converted into inalienable rights. Such has been the hardening of opinion, in the South-East in particular and encouraged by pressure groups for whom ever-present 'danger' is necessary to justify their continued existence, that Baker's successor as Environment Secretary, Nicholas Ridley, was once driven to wail despairingly, 'What's *wrong* with houses?'

Earlier I discussed the social effects and implications of this new, growing and selfish class of country-dweller, the 'squirearchy' of the late twentieth century. There are also likely to be important economic repercussions, individual and collective, from the Nimby phenomenon and the concomitant slavish adherence to and extension of planning policies founded on the situation as it was thirty or forty years ago. The first casualty is likely to be the government's rural enterprise and development programme.

'Nowadays,' says the Environment Department, 'the range of industries that can be successfully located in rural areas is expanding rapidly. There are attractions to the firms themselves in a clean and healthy environment, and there are obvious benefits to the local economy and employment.' So what sort of industries does the Department suggest? The list is short and depressing: light industry, tourism, craft workshops and recreation. Hardly the stuff, one might think, of which economic booms are made. The difficulty is that large-scale commercial growth and countryside policy as it now stands are incompatible. In 1986 the government's own Development Commission, which carries much of the responsibility for rural enterprise in England, complained bitterly that its employment programmes in the countryside were being seriously hampered by those who claimed to be its guardians. The Commission's record in 1985 was creditable enough – 337 new rural workshops built, 315 grants given for the conversion of redundant buildings in the countryside for the accommodation of new business, 20,500 small firms, employing about 100,000 people, given financial help, training or advice – but it remains a very low-level operation.

In Scotland, where development is supervised by the Scottish Office, the Scottish Development Agency established in 1985 a Rural Projects and Initiatives Unit which, among other things, operated two main schemes to encourage economic activity outside the larger centres of population and the area covered by the Highlands and Islands Development Board. One programme, known as PRIDE, offered finance in partnership with the private sector (which had to contribute at least 50 per cent) for projects 'which combine economic development with environmental improvement' and were 'primarily in the fields of crafts, tourism, other services and property improvement'. Such limits meant that there was hardly a rush to take up the offers: by the end of 1987 only thirty-six projects had been approved and a similar number remained under consideration. The second scheme, known as DRAW, was intended to establish rural workshops in the remoter areas, but again its very nature meant that any development was bound to be small. The maximum grant, excluding purchase price of land and buildings, was just £15,000 and any new building was limited to about 500 square yards. In three years, 120 projects were approved. Overall, the number of jobs created by the Scottish Development Agency in 1988 was a little more than 5500, while the number of people employed as tenants of the Agency had fallen from 49,000 in 1986–7 to 41,000. At the end of 1987, more than 300,000 men and women were unemployed in Scotland and their chances of finding jobs were estimated to be less than fifty-fifty.

The inadequacy of the programme was recognized by the government itself late in 1988 when, as a result of prompting by the Scottish branch of the Confederation of British Industry, it announced proposals for the Scottish Development Agency to be subsumed in a new body called Scottish Enterprise with a projected budget of some £500 million a year. This new agency, which would draw heavily on the experience of Scottish industrialists and businessmen, would analyse local employment needs, direct training programmes and organize sites and facilities. The Secretary of State for Scotland, Malcolm Rifkind, said that Scottish Enterprise, through a system of twenty-two local branches, would 'allow local employers and others a much greater say in the delivery of services in their area for training and enterprise creation'. At the time of writing, it was not clear whether this would mean more influence over planning decisions.

As for the Highlands and Islands Development Board, which has an annual budget of some £35 million, the record of job creation during the ten years to 1987 was 18,000, with some 6000 further jobs safeguarded through investment. The population of the Highlands and Islands is about 365,000 and the unemployment rate in February 1989 was approximately 12.5 per cent (21 per cent in the Western Isles). There have been, of course, success stories: the largest manufacturer of household chest freezers in Europe operates out of Castletown in the far north. But the lack of main roads throughout most of the Highlands and of a main-line rail network north of Inverness make life difficult for manufacturing industry and much of the Board's investment in such ventures has been recording a loss. Industries and large commercial firms that rely on technology are not well provided for, either, since there is a dearth of telephone lines modern or reliable enough to carry data-transmission and, as I write, a cellular network has yet to be established. The firms that have been attracted to the region, therefore, tend to be small and not to employ many people.

In Scotland as a whole, the jobs provided in the past by official development policies have tended to be limited in scope and also in area. North Sea oil and its related industries provide an obvious example, where employment is forecast to decline as supplies run out. There has been some growth in the electronics and electrical engineering sectors, but these have been almost all in 'Silicon Valley', between Edinburgh and Glasgow, and their volatile nature was amply demonstrated by the decision of the American electronics company Wang to pull out in 1989. The most productive area has been financial and business services, with 150,000 new jobs created by 1989, but they were virtually all in Edinburgh. What was to stop employment of that nature moving to the Highlands?

The needs are clear – motorways, main roads, rail links, a large airport, office parks, housing, shopping centres, leisure facilities. Because of the protectionist planning policy, what the Highlands has been receiving are mainly craft workshops and tourists. The

Scottish Office had placed a great deal of faith in forestry, but the conservationist furore over the afforestation of a small part of the Flow Country in Caithness, and the consequent abolition of favourable tax arrangements for private woodland, have thrown that into doubt as an important economic force in Scotland.

Much the same is true in Wales, where the Welsh Office has achieved remarkable success in attracting industry and commerce to cities in the south and to other urban areas such as Newtown and parts of North Wales, but has based its rural enterprise policy largely on farming, which has been declining, and tourism. Its Farm and Countryside Initiative, for instance, was nothing more than a short-term method of keeping busy the long-term unemployed with help from the Community Programme of the Manpower Services Commission. This gave grants for such projects as improving woodland and hedgerows, renovating old stone walls and buildings, repairing footpaths and publishing guides and local histories for the benefit of tourists. None of these things will provide proper jobs or contribute much to the economy of the principality. In the more rural counties, the rate of unemployment was running as high as 14 per cent in February 1989, often with nearly half the numbers having been out of work for more than a year. Tidying up the countryside to keep the visitors happy is hardly a realistic solution.

Indeed, tourism in general is far from the panacea that it is sometimes made out to be, though it is mentioned regularly throughout the government's literature on rural development. For one thing, the economic benefits of tourist spending may not be as valuable as the numbers of visitors suggest. To take an extreme case, the Pennine Dales 'earns' a little less than £2 a head from its million and a half tourists each year. Surveys have shown that most rural tourism in England and Wales involves outings by car of no more than twenty-five miles, and even though there has been a marked increase during recent years in country holidays, this has involved mainly the rental of cottages, caravanning and bed-and-breakfast touring, none of which does much to provide jobs. Even where employment does result from tourism, it is frequently seasonal, or part-time, or mainly in the gift-shop and hotel/catering

133

sectors. Such jobs tend to be relatively lowly paid and very far from what many people would regard as a worthwhile career.

Furthermore, tourism not only brings disadvantages with it – some parts of Southern France, Italy and Spain have had cause to regret basing their economic structures on ever growing numbers of visitors – but it is also subject to changes of fashion and circumstance, so that it is less than reliable as a foundation for long-term development. Certainly it can help, but it does not offer a credible solution unless it is used as a means of creating more permanent forms of employment. One suggestion, which has come from Wales itself, is to turn the tourist trade into an industry by acquiring manufacturing capacity to serve tourists' needs: Wales attracts many climbers and walkers, so factories could be set up there to make all-weather clothing, hiking boots, mountaineering equipment and so on. Again, though, in order for this to be achieved, some local land must be freed from planning constraints which have more to do with the view than with the welfare of the population.

There has, naturally, been some development in rural areas but this, as the Environment Department repeatedly points out (no doubt to placate the 'green' lobby which has become highly suspicious of it), has mostly affected country towns, where planning permission is more easily obtained. Apart from the obvious effects of increased congestion, what this policy has done is to export some familiar urban problems to the countryside. One manifestation of this has been mounting concern about the rising level of drunkenness and violence in what were once quiet market towns but have now assumed some of the characteristics of blighted inner cities. The planning policy has had as one of its aims the maintenance of the distinction between town and country, but it has failed to appreciate the position of the town in a predominantly rural area, which has tended to be developed in almost exactly the same way as its more suburban cousins. This is simply inappropriate, besides which the policy of restricting important development to sites within existing boundaries can, rather than improving local economic prospects, actually harm them. Such is the concern of traders in market towns that an association has been formed in the North of England to prevent and in some cases to reverse what have been described as 'alien, city-centre type schemes'. Among the 'improvements' worrying shopkeepers are:

Pedestrian precincts: One such scheme implemented in the high street of a large market town had later to be abandoned because of a disastrous falling off in trade in the main shopping area and because of the volume of complaints from nearby residents inconvenienced by extra traffic and parking in surrounding streets.

Metered parking: In some places, the amount of tourist traffic has encouraged councils to install parking meters, but this is strongly resented by residents who, of course, also have to pay for parking and who see that as amounting to a levy on attracting custom to their towns.

One-way traffic systems: Again these are the result of increasing tourist traffic, but they can cause havoc. In the city of Ripon, a one-way system had to be dismantled on the very day of its coming into operation because the city centre became completely blocked by traffic.

Traders are also wary about 'beautification' schemes and the provision of trees in the middle of small towns because what parking there is may be reduced and their businesses may suffer. Deregulation of passenger road transport may have led to a surfeit of buses in some cities, but it has done little to reverse the decline of rural services, so that people who live in the country tend to need at least one and possibly two cars. At the same time the closure of village shops in the face of price competition from supermarkets in local towns has meant that more people must now use cars to do their shopping. The loss of even a few free parking spaces can make an enormous difference to shopkeepers as potential customers give up in disgust and go elsewhere. Once you are in a car, a mile or two of extra driving makes little difference. Nor is it always easy to find vacant land in small towns to provide large car parks: the pressure became so severe in one place that market traders were even forced to pay for the privilege of parking near their stalls.

One of the founders of the anti-urbanization traders' organization, Tom Needham, from Helmsley, Yorkshire, said: 'On the one hand the council is promoting tourism at a cost of £150,000 a year. On the other hand it has introduced a new parking scheme which has discouraged regular customers. Tourists are welcome and should be encouraged, but there is a limit to the number that smaller market towns can accommodate without seriously disrupting the local way of life.' The ultimate effect of this, Needham points out, is that local businesses have to cater for a different sort of market and might well find themselves operating only during the tourist 'season', thus contributing to the decline of rural services. 'A small town where shops close down for the winter is not very attractive or good for local employment,' he said, adding that in the nearby town of Malton, shops and businesses in the marketplace had lost an estimated £100,000 worth of trade during the first month of a new pay-and-display parking system.

The results of this thoughtless and indiscriminate urban planning are more painfully obvious in the more populous South-East, where a shopping trip to somewhere such as Battle, in East Sussex, can involve quite a long wait in a queue of cars more appropriate to the West End of London. Even more dramatic is the situation in the South-West at the height of the tourist season, when some towns have to be 'closed' on certain days because they cannot accommodate any more traffic. In the summer of 1988 I noticed this phenomenon had even spread to some remote fishing villages on the Northumberland coast, particularly those on the fringes of National Trust land, where building is, of course, strictly forbidden.

The bald truth is that one cannot at the same time attempt to revive the rural economy on a less agricultural basis, encourage more people to visit the countryside and expect to retain the same number of green fields in the same places as were there before. The options are to leave the rural economy to sink, to discourage tourism or simply to change part of the basis of national planning and development regulations. The House Builders Federation is right: there is no shortage of land. Even by the conservative estimate of the National Farmers Union, five million acres of agricultural land is due to go out of production. What Britain does seem to lack is the common sense to see that some of this land must be used for building and the will to ensure that happens.

This is not to say that any sort of development or building free-for-all should be permitted and it does not mean that the countryside is about to disappear. What it does mean is that normal growth patterns should be identified, allowed for and catered to, and also that modern methods and experience must be applied. We have surely learned something during the past forty years. We need not repeat the old mistakes.

One clear lesson is that gigantism is neither necessary nor appropriate; Milton Keynes can mark the end of city-building, at least for the time being, and the Environment Department was probably right to reject plans for the large new town of Tillingham in the Green Belt east of London. Instead, it might be sensible to indulge the rural myth a little by considering the possibility of building new villages. The marked rise in the population of the countryside and the rapid inflation of property prices indicate both that many people do want to live in a rural setting and that such an ideal is more achievable than it might have been a few years ago. But a rural setting for such people means precisely what it says, not a new town set on what is called a green-field site, so why not release land for the creation of a number of new settlements of, say, up to 5000 people? They need not begin at that figure, but could be much smaller and allowed to develop to the optimum figure organically, in the way that traditional villages did.

They would be unlike old villages, however, in that they would be equipped from the outset with modern amenities: a small supermarket and perhaps other shops; a recreation centre or leisure facility; a school, pubs, a health centre and new roads built for cars rather than farm carts. If we were really ambitious we might consider limited extensions to the railway network in certain places, linking up with main-line stations, and the latest telephone equipment to cater for people working from home by computer. As in the old village, houses would be individual or in small groups, reflecting a range of needs and prices. One idea that might be imported from France is for developers to offer sites of varying sizes, equipped with water, drainage and electricity, and to let customers choose from a selection of appropriate styles of house, designed to fit in with the landscape and the appearance of nearby villages. Even if price or availability make traditional building methods impossible (their desirability is another matter), houses can be built of new materials but in traditional styles, which are generally popular because we have come to accept them as part of the view.

There are already models for this sort of development, with 'traditional'-looking houses of various styles, as would be found in old villages, built to the highest of modern standards and incorporating some of the latest technology of the construction industry. Unfortunately, most of them are not in genuinely rural areas but have been built on the fringes of existing towns as an alternative to the more usual estates of shoebox simplicity or 'executive' mock-Tudor and fake-Georgian styles. And while the houses of such 'model villages' display a pleasing eccentricity and they are arranged in a typically haphazard rural way, there is no corresponding range of prices, the average in the South-East being more than £100,000.

In 1989 plans were announced for the building of five new villages capable of accommodating up to 5000 people on sites of 400 acres yet to be chosen. These were to be for holidaymakers, however, on the model of a 'village' built in 1986 in Sherwood Forest, which now resembles nothing so much as a fun park, with its signs proclaiming 'This is Robin Hood Country'. Such developments have nothing to do with the countryside: they might as profitably be built in parkland created on derelict urban sites, since they are designed to contain within their boundaries all that the holidaymaker might need in the way of leisure facilities. All they would do, if they were ever built, would be to take up land that could be used to better advantage and to increase local traffic congestion, while providing little in the way of good jobs for rural communities or a significant contribution to their economic life. What the countryside needs is to hear more from enterprising developers who wish to build villages for people to live in.

As for existing villages and country towns, carefully controlled development, for both housing and business, should be encouraged outside existing boundaries so as to avoid the counterproductive effects I have described. A way of dealing with this would be to adopt a strict zoning policy – housing, small workshops, larger factories, office space and so on – which would mitigate the impact on the landscape by grouping necessary but 'undesirable' elements in the least favoured areas. Here again, the size, and particularly the height, of commercial development could be firmly monitored and design criteria could be enforced so that buildings would blend with both the site and the existing town.

Curiously, this simple precaution seems often to be lacking under current regulations, so that wildly unsympathetic buildings sprout in the middle of charming old market towns and even in some villages. Presumably the retention of green fields on the outskirts is considered more important as an escape from the congestion and strain of urban life. The zoning policy I have suggested could equally be applied to the new villages as they grew, so that they would become more than mere escape routes for commuters. That would present a real opportunity for the rural workshop scheme of the Development Commission and in time it might attract professional people such as lawyers and accountants to open offices.

Either of these simple ideas – or preferably both – could have far-reaching consequences for the revival of rural life and especially the declining services in country areas. Facilities provided in new villages would be used by people living in older ones and might even spread to them. The very fact of the recognition of a growing rural population would encourage the likes of banks and bus companies to exploit new markets, while the provision of new roads and other means of communication might finally persuade big business to look beyond big cities. Few have realized it yet, in Britain at least, but the information revolution will eventually make vast headquarters complexes extinct. The concept of the electronic cottage has been around for some time in Japan, where you can plug your portable computer into a public telephone, and it could well mean that the countryside becomes the place to be in the future.

The siting of such rural developments as I have outlined is important. There is no doubt, in spite of the Nimby outcry, that the South-East can accommodate some expansion, so long as it is accompanied by improvements in the infrastructure and road-building programmes more forward-looking than that which produced the infamous and inadequate M25. The real question is *whether* development should take place in the region or whether, as Michael Heseltine suggested, the quarter of a million people who currently migrate there each year should be persuaded to stay where they were. This is not only a matter of planning but also one of a wider economic strategy. As the Countryside Review Committee said in 1978, 'More co-ordination is needed in evolving policies which concern the countryside, at national level, where special inter-departmental machinery could prove valuable; at local level, where corporate management techniques could provide a useful tool; and at the intermediate level, where full advantage should be taken of the opportunities provided by the economic planning councils. More attention should be paid to the potential interactions of such policies.'

In the attempt to revitalize the inner cities, such co-operation has been established and has generally worked well, though local councils of a political complexion different from that of the government have voiced some complaints. Little such co-operation is visible in the case of rural enterprise and development, principally because the Department of the Environment has so far been bound to uphold the very planning system that inhibits development in the countryside and this has hampered the work of other government departments and regional development agencies, so that the goals of each seem sometimes to be mutually opposing. At the same time, local authorities, as they have seen other aspects of their powers eroded in the name of the government's radical reforms (not to mention its attempt to 'stamp out socialism') have clung to their structure plans even more tenaciously than before, while the National Park authorities have won for themselves increasing power over planning decisions in their areas.

When he became Environment Secretary, Nicholas Ridley, while maintaining the time-honoured stance on Green Belts and the other forms of protection, attempted to remove some of the restrictions on the development of redundant farmland and gave notice that local structure plans must become more flexible. When he insisted that the scale of development should be decided by people in the area where it was proposed, he was doing no more than voicing what amounts to current practice. Only about 2 per cent of planning applications are ever referred to the Environment Department, the rest being dealt with by local authorities. Of those that do reach the Department – usually they are the larger schemes – well over half are rejected. But Ridley's clear intention, which did not endear him either to local authorities or to the Nimby faction, was that such local decisions should be based on structure plans that take account of the wider aspects of rural policy. This is as it should be, given that the single largest obstacle to the Department's proposed scaling down of agriculture and promotion of alternative forms of rural investment is the outmoded planning system operated mostly by local councils.

Ridley also indicated that procedures under planning regulations were to be made simpler and more efficient. This is a move in the right direction, but more needs to be done. The long, complicated and costly public inquiry system that has been known to delay much-needed development for up to twenty years must be changed so that it cannot be exploited by small groups opposed for narrow or even selfish reasons to changes that will clearly benefit not only the local community as a whole but also the nation. Everyone has a right to object, but in a democracy the community has an equal right to overrule and the interests of fairness and justice are not best served in their widest sense when local decision-making can effectively be handed over to pressure groups. A system must be established whereby objections can be registered, considered and accepted or rejected quickly and the wishes of the majority taken into account.

A number of suggestions on this point have appeared in recent years. Public inquiries should operate according to a strict timetable and be limited to specific topics connected to the particular project under consideration, not to the wider questions of whether such types of development are generally good or bad. Objections should be admitted only where they refer specifically to local impact and – unless national issues are inextricably involved, as in the case of the dumping of nuclear waste, for example – they should be considered only on the basis of evidence by local individuals or organizations, and by petitions raised locally. Part of the problem with inquiries has been that local issues have been taken up as 'causes' by nationally organized pressure groups seeking to influence government policy on a wider scale. This has led to one of the quasi-rural glossy magazines running a special page in which objectors to local development plans can appeal for help from individuals or groups outside their own areas, whose only interest in such plans is to stop them being carried out anywhere. Thus the provision of a leisure centre in North Devon, or the building of a new road in Worcestershire, or the construction of new houses in Cambridgeshire are artificially inflated into matters of national interest and concern, and objectors who might not have support locally are encouraged to seek it elsewhere.

Offering advice to objectors is one thing, but mobilizing opposition among people without local interests serves only to distort the picture. It should be recognized that there is a difference between a leisure centre and a nuclear power station. For relatively small schemes, local objectors could be allowed some form of 'legal aid' so that they would not be outgunned by developers (and companies would be under the same obligation to prove their case in local terms, rather than pleading national interest or relying on outside expertise). Such a system would not be as unfair as it might appear. Local opinion would be easy to mobilize in the case of a genuinely unwanted scheme and, with the inquiry required to stick closely to the point, local knowledge on the part of objectors could have just as much weight as any so-called expertise the would-be developers might deploy.

In the case of particularly large-scale schemes, or those supported by the government, or where any public spending was involved, there have been proposals to the effect that a first requirement might be to gain the approval of Parliament for the plans involved before any local inquiry was even contemplated. Thus development would be considered in terms of the national interest, which would mean that, where it was approved by Parliament, the mind of any subsequent inquiry would be concentrated on purely local impact.

These, though, are matters of detail. Most of all, the Environment Department, as its title suggests, must take the lead in changing attitudes, exploding myths and challenging assumptions about the countryside. The Department has the power to reverse local planning decisions and, in a small way, it has begun to give notice that it is prepared to do so if its perception of the local interest differs from that of a protectionist planning authority. Greater resistance will, in the end, lead only to greater use of that central power, and that would be a pity, because change that is forced requires longer to be fully accepted. The conservation lobby must be kept firmly in its place, instead of being allowed to determine important aspects of the future of communities in which it is, at bottom, not the least interested. And the Nimbies must be shown that living in attractive surroundings is not a privilege that they can restrict to themselves. That is best done by removing the fear of change and heightening the awareness of its necessity. The old formula that development equals destruction must be clearly shown to be a mistake.

Britain might well be, as the official guide stated in 1953, one of the most densely populated areas in the world, but there remain large parts of it where the population is thinly spread. The effect of our planning policies over the past forty years has been to increase density by confining people to certain already crowded areas. The error of that approach must be admitted, as must the fact that it cannot continue. The undesirable social consequences of over-crowding are perhaps not well enough known among those fortunate enough to have more room than they need. The undesirable social consequences of mass unemployment are poss-ibly not apparent enough to well-heeled rural commuters. Instead of concentrating on the infinitesimal amount of countryside we 'lose' each year, we must recognize that there is a lot more which is being under-used or misused. Some of it should be brought out of its hypocritically and unfairly imposed quarantine to provide space, homes and jobs. That way the quality of life for all of us will ultimately be enhanced.

SIX

O'er Vales and Hills

As one who long in populous city pent,
Where houses thick and sewers annoy the air,
Forth issuing on a summer's morn to breathe
Among the pleasant villages and farms
Adjoin'd, from each thing met conceives delight.

John Milton, *Paradise Lost*

One of the strange features of recent English history is that the more urbanized society has become, the more ruralist it has pretended to be. The vast growth of cities and towns during Queen Victoria's reign shifted the whole emphasis of national life, so that it is now more than a century and a half since the average Englishman became in all essentials a townsman. Yet that process, while encouraging a dramatic decline in the rural population, did not produce a genuinely urban culture, but rather one based on the notion that urban life was no more than tolerable and demanded frequent escapes into the countryside.

This phenomenon, in fact, began to appear even while the first great expansion of urban areas was at its height. William Howitt, compiling his book *The Rural Life of England* in 1844, wrote:

It is curious to observe from the earliest hour of a Sunday morning, in fine weather, what groups are pouring into the country. There are mechanics who, in their shops and factories – while they have been caged up by their imperious necessities during the week, and have only obtained thence sights of the clear blue sky above, of the green fields laughing far away, or have only caught the wafting of a refreshing gale on their fevered cheek as they hurried homeward to a hasty meal, or back again into the incarceration of Mammon – have had their souls inflamed with desires for breaking away into the free

147

country. These have been planning, day after day, whither they shall go on Sunday. To what distant village; to what object of attraction ... Then again you see another Sunday class; tradesmen, shopkeepers and their assistants and apprentices – all those who have friends in the country – on horseback or in gigs, driving off to spend the day with those that come occasionally and pay them a visit at market and fair. The faces of these are set for farms and other country-houses within twenty miles around. There is not a horse or gig to be had for love or money at any of the livery stables on a Sunday.

They had flocked in their hundreds of thousands to seize the new opportunities offered by town and city, yet the suspicion could never be overcome that they had somehow been inveigled into a bad bargain. They might satisfy the 'imperious necessities' and receive the gifts of Mammon, but in the city they felt like slaves, tantalized in their servitude by dreams of perfect freedom in the countryside. That such freedom, including the liberty to starve, had driven them from the rural areas in the first place was conveniently obscured by a nostalgic and highly questionable sense that mankind was closest to its natural state among the woods and fields, that the real meaning of freedom was to wander at will through wide open spaces.

Following those days of early-Victorian rural jaunts, urbanization continued and spread, so that as the population increased, a greater and greater proportion of it came to regard the landscape of city and town as the inevitable one. But while urban life became the common experience, its attractions were never enough to overcome the desire to escape from its perceived disadvantages, so the assumption gradually took hold that rural interludes were essential to health and well-being. By the second quarter of the twentieth century that assumption had acquired the nature of a human right, and a popular movement gathered force to demand greater public access to the countryside.

Today, the assumption of right has taken on another characteristic, the image of a downtrodden populace rising up to reclaim an inheritance stolen by an evil landowning class. The zealots who embrace this view start from the somewhat old-fashioned premise that land is power and that in a democracy it should be, if not actually owned by the people, then at least controlled by them. Thus the environmentalist writer Marion Shoard, writing about the countryside reforms set in train by the Labour government of 1945: 'After a thousand years of oppression and exploitation in rural Britain, it looked as if the landless were at last in sight of a real share of the benefits the countryside could bestow ... this promise has been betrayed in our own era.' In her book *This Land is Our Land*, Shoard goes so far as to propose not only a tax to be levied on all land according to the extent to which it is used 'in the public interest' but also a new law that would give all citizens the right to walk anywhere they chose in the countryside, excepting land where crops were growing, or that was used for military purposes or that surrounded a house, or where there was good reason for excluding people.

Given the political implications of her writings, one might sympathize with Shoard, even if not agreeing with her, if she suggested that all land should be nationalized. If land represents power, it is only because it is a resource, and if it is a resource it confers not only benefits but also responsibility. In those circumstances, there may well be a case for public ownership of land in a democratic society. But Shoard falls into the muddled thinking that is characteristic of an urban society when it meddles uncomprehendingly and, what is worse, sentimentally in the countryside that it has left. Her view, and that of many like her, is essentially an urban one: the countryside is only a resource insofar as what it looks like – 'landscape' rather than 'countryside' is the fashionable term today – and only a benefit in terms of the use to which it can be put for leisure purposes. Thus the people should not have the right to own the land, but only to walk about in it and look at it: power without responsibility. The idea that land not built on is there to be played on is one born not in the countryside but in the city park, just as the modern notion of 'animal rights' comes from the zoo rather than the farmyard. As a place to live and work in, the countryside is under greater threat from the urban misconceptions of Shoard and her kind than from all the bulldozers in Britain.

To begin with, the language of such people is that of conflict. Shoard's book was subtitled *The Battle for Britain's Countryside* and she wrote of 'hostility towards the landowning classes', of 'two different value systems on course for collision', of 'a determined onslaught', an 'impending clash' and 'battle-lines'. The countryside is seen as something to be fought over, and indeed Shoard described land as always having been the subject of struggle between tribes and races, nations and classes who wished to put it to different uses. This, as I have already pointed out, is a somewhat outdated view. A study of modern history indicates quite clearly that ideology, whether religious or political, is the basis of almost all serious human conflict: territory is merely the external manifestation of opposing views, meaning absolutely nothing by itself, other than in symbolic terms. In fact, land and its ownership are probably less important now than they have ever been as sources of power. The technological and communications revolution through which we are passing places the battle lines not on the ground but in the mind. Shoard acknowledged as much with her reference to 'two different value systems', yet she and others persist in pursuing physical solutions to intellectual problems. Punitive legislation against the 'selfish' landowners and the unleashing of the entire population to wander at will in the countryside would only harden unhelpful attitudes on both sides, when what is required, if rural Britain is to have a healthy future, is to change them.

One of the least helpful attitudes on the urban side of the conflicting value systems is the one that places the recreational value of the countryside above all else. Even the Countryside Review Committee, which for the most part was notable for its lack of prejudice, simply accepted the assumption that recreational needs were 'a key element in discussion on the long-term future of our rural areas', a hypothesis apparently based on nothing more than the fact that 'today, more people ... have more leisure time than ever before' and that 'the countryside is now used for recreation on a massive scale'. Since the Committee wisely pointed out that more than 80 per cent of such recreational demand came from townspeople and that 'we need to think in terms of dealing with this partly at source', a closer questioning of the suitability of the countryside as a site for mass recreation might have been in order, but by the 1970s the assumption was too well founded to be seriously challenged.

To its credit, however, the Committee did draw attention to the potential for 'a very wide range of conflict' in the growing urban demand for rural recreation:

People all too often leave gates open, letting sheep and cattle stray, or drop dangerous litter, or trample crops. In dry summers the fire risk is great. Furthermore, when large numbers of people congregate in a particular area where planned facilities are inadequate, trespass may be common and annoyance and financial loss to farmers are aggravated ...

Leisure activities can also affect scenery and wildlife. Clearly, for instance, excessive concentrations of visitors in particular areas undoubtedly add to the problems and the costs of preserving landscapes. In the end, there may be irreparable damage. The movement of people may erode natural surfaces, or walls may be broken down and hedges spoilt. Visitors can also create eyesores: parked cars, caravans or tents and litter. The more active can wear away mountain paths, rock faces or lake and river banks. The noise generated by some sports – the use of power boats on lakes is one example – can disturb the very quietness which others wish to find.

Recreation in the countryside centres on communities ... however, it is just as true of rural England as elsewhere in the world that in adapting to the visitor local communities may be changed beyond recognition. Although some residents may welcome the bustle and 'life' which visitors bring ... most will be much more aware of the lost amenity and social disruption which results. In extreme cases visitors may prove to be the predominant partners in the relationship and the local community become dependent on them, to its loss.

In the decade following the Committee's deliberations, none of these problems was seriously considered. The emphasis remained on urban rather than rural needs, and ever larger numbers of people were encouraged to spend their leisure time in the countryside, partly to justify the increasing demands for conservation, on the premise that the more public interest was generated the easier it would be to slap some sort of preservation order on more and more 'heritage' landscape.

The devastation of the Three Peaks footpaths, which I discussed earlier, was only one result of this growing urban domination and a new conflict began to arise, between the conservation and the public access lobbies. In 1988 the Council for the Protection of Rural England felt moved to criticize the city of Bradford for its 'success' in attracting visitors to the legendary Ilkley Moor, the 3840 acres of which is owned by the local authority. 'The moor is suffering from over-popularity,' said a local official of the CPRE, bemoaning the damage caused by an estimated quarter of a million annual visitors. Not only were paths being destroyed, as in the Three Peaks, but people were also 'straying' on to open moorland and trampling down vegetation. Moreover, the area was becoming an eyesore because of litter, a sad fate for what one local activist described, predictably, as 'the heritage of all Yorkshiremen'. The Yorkshiremen and others were, it seemed, taking their heritage too much for granted, prompting the CPRE to demand that tourists should be kept off the moor 'for as long as it takes' to allow its return to a state appropriate to a piece of heritage. (The response of the Council, incidentally, was illuminating. In answer to criticism of a failure to provide litter bins, a spokesman said there was a very good reason for that – they tended to attract litter.)

Inevitably, the law of double standards was soon brought into play. The Duke of Devonshire, who is responsible for attracting some 300,000 visitors a year to his stately home at Chatsworth in Derbyshire, complained that 'There is clearly a clash of interest between those who live and work within' the boundaries of the Peak National Park 'and those who come to visit an area of outstanding natural beauty'. With fine irony, his comments appeared in a magazine called *Country Homes and Interiors*, one of the self-appointed flagships of designer ruralism for urban audiences. For irony, though, it would be difficult to surpass a donation made to the funds of the Lake District Appeal, which is intended to make good the damage done in the area by mass tourism. The contribution came from a company called Moorland Publishing, which owes its existence to the business of selling Lake District guides to the very visitors who have made the appeal necessary, directing them to the places likeliest to be damaged.

The fundamental dilemma of public access to the countryside was summed up in 1989 by a member of the Association of Friends of Cannock Chase, a 26-square-mile corner of Staffordshire that forms the smallest Area of Outstanding Natural Beauty in Britain, and that contains within its borders no fewer than 34 car parks: 'The problem is that we invite the world and his wife, and his children, and his dog, and his car, who then destroy what they have come to see.' The Chase, a wild area of heath and forest, receives about half a million visitors a year and, to add to its attraction to the town-dwellers of the West Midlands, it contains a 3000-acre country park, a designation nicely illustrating the urban overtones of modern rural appellation: a park, after all, is now accepted as a place where one goes to enjoy oneself. The area is administered by Staffordshire County Council, which, according to the Friends of Cannock Chase, has seen its basic role as attracting 'more and more people to come from farther and farther afield'. The secretary of the Association complained: 'There are too many visitors, and things are made too easy for them.' Yet how can one preserve the countryside for the benefit of the public and then make it difficult for the public to see it?

And in spite of such acknowledgement of the difficulties and damage that can result from mass tourism, the demands for greater access to the countryside by more people continue to increase. One of the loudest voices in this respect is that of the Ramblers Association, which was formed in the 1930s in an atmosphere of protest against restrictive practices by country landowners. The Association is based not in some rural haven but, of course, in London, and of its 250 or so affiliated rambling clubs, 10 per cent are to be found in the Greater London area. Its 68,000 members do not all live in towns, but it appears in its attitude as essentially an organization dedicated to the needs mainly of urbanites who enjoy

153

walking, an activity pursued by an average of four million people every week. Countryfolk in general do not need the help of organizations that will point them in the direction of good walks.

Now walking is undoubtedly a simple and splendid form of exercise, and throughout Britain there are thousands of miles of pavements on which one might walk at will, untroubled by thoughts of trespassing, with a multitude of interesting things to see, no shortage of places in which to take refreshment, and unlimited opportunities to observe the lives of different communities and even to exchange a few words with some of their members. This, however, will not do for the rambler, whose aim is to place himself as far away from people as possible, to gaze not at varied and interesting buildings but at empty spaces and, most of all, to walk not just on land where he has a perfect right to be but specifically where he has no right to be. The rambler insists on dressing up in waterproof clothing, heavy boots and thick socks (red is the most popular colour, I have observed), seizing a map in a clear plastic cover and striking out into the wilderness, complaining all the while about blocked footpaths, fences, 'alien' conifers, 'unsightly' farm buildings, signs saying 'Private', quarries, and the general lack of care and consideration shown by countryfolk towards their precious environment. The rambler, in other words, is a landscape consumer.

During my time living in the Yorkshire Dales, I watched innumerable ramblers trudging mournfully through my village and along well-worn footpaths (the least used and most interesting walks were known only to locals and often did not appear on the plastic-covered maps), and I reached the conclusion that they were happiest when the weather was as its most foul. The greatest numbers would generally be seen on days when most sensible Dalespeople would not set foot out of doors, barring dire necessity. I assumed this at least justified what must be a fairly considerable investment in waterproof clothing. Such eccentricity would be harmless enough were it not for the fact that it has become not only a form of mass recreation, as I have indicated (and in principle there is nothing remotely wrong with that), but also a movement of mass protest. According to a past president of the Ramblers

his is planning policy: a
urban-style detached house
 inappropriately in the
ldle of a Cambridgeshire
age, while a shopping centre
re suited to a city centre
npletely changes the atmos-
re of a Sussex market town

The rush to realize the modern rural dream has meant that agricultural buildings never intended for habitation now sell to house-hunters for £100,000 or more – and then there are the effort and cost of restoration

Some rural housing development manages to capture the true feeling of the traditional village, such as this new 'hamlet' in Kent. The problem is that the price of such houses puts them well beyond the reach of many of the indigenous rural population

Resistance to change in the countryside has led to what is known as the 'Nimby' syndrome – Not In My Back Yard. The need for more roads in Britain is obvious, but many people seem to prefer traffic jams to the loss of favourite pieces of country-side. On the other hand, rural residents sometimes *do* have cause for complaint when change overtakes them, as the signs in Hangman's Wood demonstrate

Economic development or eyesore? This cement works in Weardale might not do much for the landscape, but it is a valuable source of employment in an area where jobs are hard to come by and depopulation has been severe. People must be taken into account in rural planning, and conservation is not always preferable to development

In the past people had country houses, but to British ears attuned to the softest of social nuances 'country houses' means something more specific: 'country homes' are what most people buy in these supposedly more egalitarian times

Ramblers in full cry: about four million people in Britain go walking in the countryside every week, but too often the perceptions they take with them are essentially urban

Horse society: more than three million people in Britain now ride regularly

Above: An entire industry has grown up on the basis of 'our heritage' and one of its effects has been to associate the countryside firmly with the past

The weekend exodus to the countryside is nothing new, as this nineteenth-century engraving shows, but nowadays visitors include those who like to play war games

Signs of the times: in some places the countryside seems to take on the characteristics of subtopia as a multiplicity of notices exhorts, informs and occasionally entertains. The pleasure-park aspect of rural development betrays the urban roots of what passes for a policy on the countryside

Association, Mike Harding – who does actually live in the country – the 'major' work of the organization is 'keeping the footpaths open and getting new ones dedicated, and fighting for access to moorlands and the mountains of these islands'. The language of conflict again.

To this end the Association organizes events such as the Forbidden Britain Day, which drew attention to thirty places throughout the country where people wished to walk but were prevented from doing so. Among the sites claimed by the rebellious ramblers were land owned by the Yorkshire Water Authority in the Brontë country on the borders of Yorkshire and Lancashire; a 120-acre stretch of Oxfordshire woodland which is customarily opened to the public on one day a year; and – most hated of all – land in 'beauty spots' owned by the Ministry of Defence. One such was Mickle Fell, an army training range in the midst of the newly designated North Pennines Area of Outstanding Natural Beauty. The fell is near High Force, reckoned by some people to be the largest waterfall in England, where there is already a good deal of walking room at what has been for many years a popular attraction for visitors and locals alike. Not enough room for the Ramblers Association, however, in spite of the fact that their precious Pennine Way is also close by. 'An outrage' was how one militant described the fact that he was not permitted to scale at will the 2600 feet of Mickle Fell, apparently on the presumption that anything you see you should be able to walk on. At another time there was a mass trespass in the Peak National Park, resulting in sometimes violent confrontation with gamekeepers and policemen on what was, after all, private land. In 1989, the Ramblers Association launched an appeal fund aiming to raise £40,000 to allow it to continue 'to fight the footpath cause' and to press for a large increase in the not inconsiderable sum of £12 million already being spent on maintaining rural rights of way.

Quite why the countryside should be open to all comers the Ramblers, like Marion Shoard, can explain only vaguely, muttering about their heritage (inevitably) and birthright. When they complain about lack of access to land that is publicly owned, they have a case, but to them, it seems, the distinction between public space and private property, so obvious in urban areas, does not apply outside city limits.

Perhaps this is because, if Harding is to be believed, Ramblers do not much like anybody who has any responsibility for the countryside. Apart from landowners themselves, National Park authorities, the Forestry Commission, commercial forestry companies and farmers are particular targets. 'My main interest is the National Parks because of the disastrous state they're in at the moment,' Harding said. 'They were designed as the "lungs of the nation" and any development would be at local level and consistent with the nature of the parks, but development has gone on piecemeal and ignored the original ideas. In Ribblesdale there are something like four quarries in a six-mile range. They've blasted away the landscape leaving massive scars. We've got quarrying, the Forestry Commission and the Economic Forestry group – they're the biggest villains.' As for farmers, they are the ones who most often want footpaths blocked, rerouted or discontinued. Worse still, they behave in a manner that does not accord with landscape consumption. 'I am not allowed to alter the shape of my windows because it may be inconsistent with the local architecture, but Fred Giles, farmer, can put up massive aluminium silos, concrete bunkers, cowhouses, asbestos roofs, and of any size, too.'

Again, the urban prejudices and failure to understand the countryside are clear. To listen to Harding, one would think that Farmer Giles put up his buildings out of sheer cussedness, for the sole purpose of spoiling the landscape. The probability that he is not going to build anything that he does not need for his business does not enter the argument. And while Harding is right to criticize the often pettifogging planning restrictions in force in National Parks, there must surely be a distinction between those who live in the countryside purely out of choice (Harding earns his living as a comedian and writer) and those like Farmer Giles who live there because it is their job. As for the quarrying and the forestry, where else are their products to come from if not from the countryside? And if the countryside is not to be used for economic purposes, what else is it to be used for? Without some form of economic activity the countryside would be nothing more than what so many of the urban recreationists imagine it to be – a pleasure park.

But farmers are certainly not the only individuals who excite the ire of the Ramblers Association. In 1989 one group of members passed a resolution condemning what it called the new common practice among buyers of country houses to close or divert public rights of way on their land. A member of the council of the Association, Kate Ashbrook, said vehemently: 'We deplore the way new landowners try to tamper with public highways for their private convenience. Too often we find that, no sooner has someone bought a residential property than he applies to have a path over his land closed or moved. His reasons are often that the path is "a threat to his security" or "an intrusion on his privacy", but there is no evidence that such allegations are true. In any case the path was there long before he was, and he can have no excuse for not having known when he bought the land that there was a path across it.

'What these selfish owners want is to increase the value of their properties by removing what are probably very ancient public paths across them. These people want to live in the country, but on their own terms. They want to change the countryside's traditions and history and to deny people their lawful enjoyment of the landscape.'

Such is the view typical of the Ramblers Association, but it is one that bears some examination. To begin with, one might think that a resident would have a better idea than a weekend walker of what might constitute a threat to his security or an intrusion on his privacy – and even where these do not in practice exist at the moment, the fact that a householder perceives them to be present is important for his peace of mind. As I know from personal experience of living in remote rural districts, not only can it be unnerving to encounter strange groups of people wandering near one's house, but also not all walkers are as scrupulous as Ramblers may be in restricting their peregrinations to designated rights of way. The inquisitive often deliberately deviate in order to look at a house, even – as has happened with me – stopping to peer in through windows, and more than once I have found picnickers sprawled across private access. Even when deviations are not deliberate, many 'amateur' walkers stray from public footpaths through ignorance or lack of care.

A second point to be borne in mind is that ancient public footpaths were most often established for a purpose, as a means for local people to take shortcuts to church or village, farm or water supply. They were not simply provided for 'lawful enjoyment of the landscape'. In most cases, the original justification for a public right of way across private land has long since disappeared, so that the use of such a footpath has now assumed the character more of a privilege than a right. Walkers, after all, are merely filling their leisure time.

I would agree that it might be seen as sheer bloody-mindedness to seek to close a public footpath for no good reason other than that the landowner does not like it. I cannot, however, accept that a simple diversion is such a crime, even if it is just for the convenience of the owner. People who actually live in the countryside, and have paid money to do so, have rights and privileges which are just as worthy of protection as those of people whose rural interests are predominantly recreational – and also cost them nothing.

Yet because the majority of the population spends most of its life in towns and cities, it is the urban view of the rural leisure resource that is inexorably gaining ground. The Ramblers Association has been joined by other groups in its protests against what it sees as unjust exclusion. One militant organization is currently demonstrating on behalf of a public right of access to grouse moors, which it sets out to invade on 12 August, the day the grouse season opens. Another is called CRACK, the Campaign for River Access for Canoes and Kayaks, which employs guerilla tactics against both anglers and riparian landowners in an attempt to gain more miles of waterways for its sport. 'The rivers are the heritage of everyone,' a CRACK spokesman said shortly after the formation of the group in 1986. That being the case, CRACK holds sail-ins on rivers normally reserved for anglers, the concept of heritage, apparently, not extending to the people who actually own the waterways and so, under the law, have the right to let them be used by whomever they see fit.

All this clamour for public access is not as altruistic as it might seem. The walking fraternity, for example, having campaigned vigorously and continuing to 'fight' for the public's rights of way in the countryside, is not at all pleased when members of the public try to use their rights of way for purposes other than those approved of by walkers. The growing sports of off-road motor-cycling and the hill-racing of four-wheel-drive vehicles have been attacked with increasing bitterness in recent years by ramblers, who complain about 'the shattered tranquillity of the unlucky walker' and express the hope that 'this selfish activity will be stopped' or even that some parts of the countryside, such as National Parks, should be 'pedestrianized'. (As a footnote, it is interesting to remark that 'selfish' appears to be a favourite term of abuse among competing groups of contemporary country-lovers: not only is it applied to farmers, landowners, householders, anglers, and motor-sport enthusiasts, but it has also been levelled at what would seem on the face of it to be the ecologically sound pursuit of clay pigeon shooting, a correspondent to *Country Homes and Interiors* bewailing that 'the noise, irritation and unpleasantness affect everyone but the sport's selfish participants'. Perhaps this is just a development of the language, with 'selfish' evolving as a simple description of a person whose interests or hobbies are different from one's own.)

Nor is the public access brigade entirely delighted when its propaganda is successful enough to stimulate interest on a large scale, even in its own particular sphere of activity. The magazine *The Great Outdoors*, for instance, sniped at 'suburbanization of the countryside' when, to encourage more public access to walks, Scottish Conservation Projects began providing refuges and information centres on part of the 212-mile Southern Upland Way. The magazine sarcastically supposed that 'it's only a matter of time before we get a tarmaced surface and cycle hire centres to further aid those poor weary walkers.' Some militants have gone so far as to suggest that public footpaths in the most rugged countryside should be deliberately left in poor repair so as to discourage people other than those considered 'bona fide' walkers. It does not seem to have occurred to the complainers that you cannot in all sincerity constantly demand the freeing of more countryside for people to use in their leisure hours, on the ground that it is their right and heritage, and then try to stop them exercising the liberty you claim to be winning for them. Or are we to have a new and privileged class of licensed countryside-consumers? Fortunately, there remain enough sensible ruralists who condemn the fanatics as 'eco-fascists'.

All this mania for leisure space in the countryside has one especially interesting feature that gives the lie to the talk of heritage and tradition: that is, it does not extend to certain activities traditionally associated with rural life – 'blood sports' as their growing numbers of critics call them; 'field sports' as their adherents reply defensively. These were not mentioned in the discussion paper *Leisure and the Countryside* produced by the Countryside Review Committee, and so far as many of the part-time ruralists are concerned, they are utterly unmentionable except in terms of abuse. Notwithstanding some reports of a revival of cockfighting, badger-baiting and dog-fighting promoted by newly countrified yuppies, there is a growing tendency among modern urban country-lovers to regard some aspects of 'our rural heritage' as morally wrong, notably foxhunting.

There has, of course, been opposition to hunting for years. For some it has conscientious roots, accompanying vague liberal urges that may include antipathy towards eating meat, a fondness for yoghurt and muesli, serious concern for civil rights and a regular order for the *Guardian*. Others see it in terms of social class: those who keep horses and have both the time and the money to hunt are the despised remnants of an old, oppressive ruling élite. Woolly liberalism on the one hand and a form of class envy on the other have given rise to groups of hunt saboteurs, who have become a regular feature and added to the sport at meets in various parts of the country. A new dimension to the opposition was created in 1983 when the Labour Party included a commitment to abolish hunting with hounds in its election manifesto, a promise that has remained part of Labour policy ever since. This development had nothing directly to do with the countryside; Labour's roots are predominantly urban and industrial and it was attempting to appeal to urban voters – a fact betrayed by its failure to comment on another bloodsport, angling, which seems to be ideologically sound because it has traditionally offered healthy leisure hours to the industrial working classes. Another significant feature was the fact that the section of the manifesto dealing with hunting failed to understand, as only a townsman would, why and how it is practised.

More notable still, though, was that before the 1987 election the hunting fraternity felt compelled to respond to the challenge. There are some 200 packs of hounds in Britain, many of them with substantial waiting-lists for hunt membership, and more than a million people hunt regularly. These are large numbers, and a not inconsiderable proportion of them are people who have no connections with the squirearchy, but such has been the climate of opinion in recent years that the British Equestrian Trade Association and the British Field Sports Society (with the support of five million members) could not ignore the threat. Another example of the gap between rural and urban thinking became another area of conflict.

The hunters attempted to divert the attention of the public at large away from the 'humanitarian' arguments of the critics and towards economic and other matters. The British Equestrian Association produced a report stating that if hunting with horses and hounds was abolished, its members would lose £47 million in turnover and some 340 small firms would face bankruptcy. At least 5500 full-time jobs would be lost in the manufacturing of saddlery, veterinary supplies, provision of forage, farriers and specialists in horse transport. To this other interested parties added people employed in hunt kennels and stables, bringing the total number of jobs at risk to some 18,500 full-time and about 4700 part-time. These, it was felt, were the sort of terms that urbanites would understand. But then the hunting lobby could not resist the temptation to overstate its case, with results that were less than satisfactory.

It was pointed out, for example, that Britain had the biggest and most thriving fox population in Europe. That seemed to sit uncomfortably with the common rationale that hunting is an efficient and relatively humane way of controlling foxes. As the distinguished editor of *Horse and Hound*, Michael Clayton, put it:

'Culling with hounds with officially registered packs observing a strict code of conduct is infinitely preferable to ... "disorganised" hunting ... It would be impossible to police adequately the huge increase in hunting with snares, poisons and inefficient shooting that would result ...' Yet if culling with hounds results in the healthiest population of foxes in Europe, it can hardly be said to be an efficient means of control, so why should its abolition make any difference to the extent of other measures used against foxes? It might have been better to cite the current state of the British fox as a justification for the other frequently quoted defence, that hunting is not inhumane because foxes are hardly ever caught.

Another claim made on behalf of huntin' folk was that a ban would drive to the brink of extinction one of the best types of riding horse in the world and reduce hounds to the status of zoological specimens. Again this is highly questionable. If the main pleasure in the sport is derived from riding hunters, that could equally be achieved by drag-hunting, as is practised in the United States, which would also keep the hounds active. In any case, badgers are no longer commonly hunted, but the dachshund survives outside zoos; the 'French' poodle was originally a German hunting dog and flourishes mightily in a milieu far removed from its traditional role, as do beagles, bassett-hounds and a variety of terriers. The vision that a ban on hunting would mean the end of civilization as we know it is not exactly credible. Equally unhelpful was the statement made by the chairman of the British Field Sports Society, Sir Stephen Hastings, who forecast that the Labour commitment would lead to 'anarchy and violence in the country-side and the random pursuit of quarry' – to its critics that might sound like an accurate description of foxhunting.

As it happened the Labour Party lost the 1987 election for reasons that did not have much to do with its attitude towards foxhunting, or the hunting fraternity's unimpressive defence of it, but a perhaps more worrying sign of new ruralist thinking came the following year when the National Trust was infiltrated by scores of anti-hunting activists who forced a note on a motion to ban the sport from the Trust's half a million acres in England, Wales and Northern Ireland. The proposal was heavily defeated, but it offers another illustration of the way in which the rural heritage industry can be exploited for sectarian purposes.

In truth, the only sound case to be presented in favour of foxhunting is that a very large number of people enjoy it, which means that the argument for retaining it (leaving aside the 'humanitarian' aspect, which is really nothing more than a red-herring) is the same as that for allowing rambling, canoeing, angling, moto-cross, cycle-racing, hang-gliding and all the other activities that people like to pursue in the countryside. Either we accept the idea of the rural pleasure park or we do not, and if it is accepted then we must beware of making ideological distinctions between those who might and might not be allowed to use it. If walkers were to be permitted virtually unrestricted access, then why should horse-riders (of whom there are currently about three million) not claim the same right, or fishermen, or shooting enthusiasts, or people who like to race four-wheel-drive vehicles over fields and up hillsides? Of course that would be ridiculous, turning the countryside into more of a fairground than a park and ensuring that our fabled heritage was not left to us for long. Yet there is no rationale for giving ramblers, say, the freedom to follow their sectional interest at random if the same liberty is not accorded to other groups: as we have seen in the cases of the Three Peaks and Ilkley Moor, rambling is not an entirely harmless pursuit and an enormous amount of damage can be caused by far fewer than four million walkers. Public access means access for all, access that must inevitably be shared, and those who raise it as a battle-cry should take good care to know what precisely they are campaigning for.

Surely the only acceptable course, to avoid exposing the country-side to needless abuse and to prevent conflict among the multi-farious special-interest groups, is to provide certain areas for particular activities. When people wish to play tennis, they go to a place specifically designed for that purpose – and nobody has ever suggested that, say, the whole of Birmingham should be turned into a gigantic tennis court. Why should it be any different in the countryside? It cannot be repeated too often that there is enough space in the countryside to accommodate competing claims on its use, so long as that space is controlled, developed and managed carefully, and so long as it is clear that no one group of enthusiasts has a monopoly on the land that is available. It must also be realized that any activity in the countryside is going to change it, if not 'damage' it, and that such change and decay is part of a process that began long before people thought of rural areas as leisure facilities.

Sport and leisure comprise one aspect of the resources available to us in the countryside, but only one. It must not be allowed to take precedence over others. Ramblers may be right to campaign to keep footpaths open and even to press for the opening of new ones, if the present network of more than 130,000 miles really is insufficient to meet the demand, but there should be no presumption that they are right and there is no reason why their perceived needs should be given priority. Nor, for the same reason, is there any justification for the Ramblers Association to present itself as a guardian of rural heritage: given the reason for its existence, it is always going to be biased. Development in the countryside cannot be decided on the basis of whether it will spoil a fleeting view for people enjoying a stroll. Indeed the connection between rambling and rural preservation is a false one, invented, I suspect, mainly for the purpose of supporting walkers' demands for ever wider access.

The same is true of other groups with particular interests, including in some respects those whose chief concern is what they call conservation. What they are doing is seeking to impose their own narrow views on people whose needs and perceptions may be different. As an example, the walkers, climbers and conservationists who, in 1989, were mobilizing to oppose the development of a ski resort at Ben Wyvis, north of Inverness, did so on the ground that 'yet another Scottish mountain is under threat from development and another unspoiled landscape is set to be defiled for private gain'. Private gain, perhaps, but what about the gain for the increasing numbers of people who enjoy skiing? Not every mountain in Scotland is going to be turned into a resort, and every landscape could be said to be defiled the moment a human being puts it to his own use – even if he does no more than walk in it.

Finally, there is absolutely no convincing case to be made for the suspension of property rights in the countryside on the basis that people from the towns are more deserving than those seen as fortunate enough to have the benefits of rural life on their doorsteps, or even less in the name of some hazy notion of pre-feudal paradise. Land that is publicly owned is another matter entirely, though, and pressure should be applied on the state both to produce incontestable reasons why it must exclude people from areas which it holds on their behalf and to use some of the revenues from the taxes it collects for the purpose of providing more rural amenities for those who pay them.

In fact, there is a strong case for the government to take an altogether firmer grip on the use of the countryside for leisure activities if, as its literature on rural enterprise suggests, tourism is considered to be an important element in future development. By the mid-1980s Britain was earning upwards of £12,000 million a year from tourism by both foreign visitors and British residents, much of it based in rural areas. But while the British Tourist Authority was busily promoting our national attractions abroad and the tourist boards of England, Scotland, Wales and Northern Ireland were doing their best to persuade more natives to explore the British Isles, the organization, direction and management of tourism remained for the most part amateurish and ad hoc in the time-honoured British tradition. Moreover, little thought appeared to be given to means of absorbing growing numbers of tourists, how and where any but the most basic facilities might be provided for them and how their impact on the country might be managed, especially in the rural areas that are least equipped to deal with them.

Part of the reason for this, no doubt, is a certain ambivalence towards tourists on the part of the British, which probably stems from a long period in which they were more accustomed to being the visitors than the visited. While many welcome the income and employment tourism can generate (it is estimated that getting on for one and a quarter million people now work in the tourist industry in Britain), others with more refined sensibilities equate the tourist with crassness and ignorance, silly questions and disc cameras, fish and chips and coach outings. Such disdain manifests itself in the number of Britons today who buy not holidays but holiday homes, whether they be in Tuscany or Cornwall, in order to claim affiliation which, they fondly believe, removes the embarrassing tourist label. It also extends to the tourists who arrive in Britain. Not long ago it was fashionable in London to wear a badge proclaiming 'I'm Not a Tourist – I Live Here', while more recently a writer in the liberal-minded *Guardian* waxed cynical over the fact that in the Yorkshire Dales 'publicity officers are springing up in every town and district, and holiday cottage rental – I almost said racket – is enjoying a boom'. It is perhaps hardly surprising that there is in Britain a degree of reluctance to take tourism quite as seriously as some other European countries do.

In rural areas themselves, tourists tend to attract rather less suspicion than incomers, mainly because their impact is rather more superficial. On the other hand, there are frequently negative reactions to the introduction of tourist-oriented changes. Looking back over more than a decade of writing a weekly column for a rural newspaper, one man wrote: 'Even within the last twelve years the expansion of the volume of vehicles in our lanes has been dramatic ... Quiet and secluded places I knew as a child are now beauty spots with picnic areas and car parks and I find it quite remarkable that the countryside through which I roamed as free as the wild life itself, is now marked with signs defining footpaths, picnic areas, car parks, toilets and information centres. Moorland paths are now wide open highways.' In a world whose only certainty is change, it would be somewhat unreasonable to expect places to remain just as they were when one was a child, but a more co-ordinated and professional approach to dealing with tourism might find a way of responding to the changes it brings more gently and with greater sensitivity. A small yellow circle denoting a footpath, for instance, is greatly preferable to a large wooden sign of the sort generally found, bearing legends such as 'Dunroamin', in suburban garden-centres. Better footpath maps and booklets containing unmistakable directions would also help to reduce the necessity of sign-posting. There is no good reason why visitor centres should be sited anywhere near the scenic attractions to which they refer: tourists could obtain all the information they required in the nearest town, before setting off for the beauty-spot of their choice.

Car parks and traffic in general are much more serious problems, and there are no easy solutions. The areas most appreciated tend to be those that are most remote, which makes reaching them difficult without a car, and the fact is that most British visitors take their countryside in small doses and fairly short distances, so their tourism is likely to be directly from home by car. This can make life hell for the country-dweller. I know from personal experience the frustration that can arise from a drive to the nearest shop, when one is forced to crawl along behind convoys of motorized sightseers afraid of narrow roads and unexpected bends, though paying more attention to the scenery than the road and likely to stop without warning should a gateway appear that affords an interesting view. What makes it worse is the number of people who 'consume' the countryside without apparently ever leaving their cars. I have often been astonished at the sight of cars parked by the side of a country road, their occupants inside them on a beautiful summer's day and reading newspapers. So much for healthy fresh air.

But this is actually one case in which urban solutions are appropriate to the countryside. Traffic management schemes have been forced on cities and towns by the increased volume of vehicles and I do not see why, suitably ruralized, similar systems cannot be applied on the country roads most used by tourists: local residents could have stickers on their cars (like those for disc-parking in country towns) indicating that restrictions did not apply to them. The basis of parking could be altered from one of anywhere that is not forbidden to one of nowhere that is not expressly allowed. Some roads could be set aside for the use of residents only, others could be closed to coaches. Where present roads are clearly inadequate, new ones should be built with tourist traffic specifically in mind, though they may also prove to be of benefit to locals out of season – twisting lanes are all very nice until one needs to go somewhere in a hurry. Proper landscaping could minimize or even neutralize the visual effect where scenery was considered to be of prime importance. Better still, in particularly sensitive areas the use of cars could be discouraged by the provision of minibus shuttle services where the distances involved precluded walking, a rural version of the urban 'park and ride' schemes.

At the root of the need for such special measures, of course, is overcrowding, the tendency for tourists to huddle together in the country just as they do in towns. The Countryside Review Committee commented: 'It seems likely that people's choice of destination is largely determined by fashion and publicity.' Quite so. It seems likely that a large part of the entire phenomenon of new ruralism is determined by fashion and publicity, which is why, though it must obviously be taken account of, we should be wary of using it as a basis for long-term decisions about the future of the countryside. The Committee went on: 'This means that many sites which are potentially attractive remain under-used.' There have been changes in the past decade, occasioned partly by the sheer pressure of numbers, so that tourist activity is more widely spread, but still it is the well-known areas, such as the Lake District, that bear the brunt of the annual invasion. Here again a more co-ordinated and better-directed approach could help to relieve problems, directing attention to less crowded regions and influencing fashion through publicity, as is done in the market for foreign holidays, where 'new' destinations are eagerly sought.

Above all, though, what is required is a revision of attitudes towards tourism in general and rural tourism in particular. Greater leisure and increasing mobility almost certainly mean that demand will continue to grow for the foreseeable future and all the indications are that tourism will have an important bearing on the development of the countryside, for good or ill. I have referred elsewhere to the uncertainty of its economic benefits in rural areas, but this arises partly from the present lack of organization and partly from the ambivalent attitude towards the whole business. It may have something to do with folk memories of master–servant relationships, but whatever the reason the English in particular are not proud of any skills they might have in catering to the needs of people with leisure time and the money to indulge themselves (try to find a good restaurant with a staff of English waiters). The Irish and Scots are better, no doubt because their traditions of hospitality are stronger. In general, the status of the hotel and catering trades and similar service industries is far too low, as is the pay. This has led to something of a bias against these occupations as a career, though attitudes have softened a little in the face of the resurgence of mass unemployment for the first time since the 1930s. Very often people who work in restaurants and hotels feel the need to excuse themselves by saying that the job is only temporary, that they are doing it only until they can find something 'better'.

An industry that helps to earn for the nation more than £12,000 million a year deserves greater recognition and respect, including self-respect, and while the standards of catering and service in Britain still have some way to go before they reach those of, say, the French and the Italians, they have improved markedly during the past twenty years, and that should be acknowledged and built on. In part this means stripping tourism of its fish-and-chips image, recognizing that there is a broad market to be exploited. Too often the tourist facilities that are provided – and heaven knows they are little enough – are basic and tatty and put off the people with most money to spend. Already some disaffected farmers have seen the potential of the luxury market and converted their holdings into country-house hotels, but more establishments of the highest standards are needed, as are more and better restaurants. The countryside is not all about mud, wellington boots, discomfort and butane stoves in the lay-bys.

It is not all about day-trippers, either. If tourism is to bring real benefit to rural communities and at the same time to help to maintain the special qualities of country life, the holiday market must be exploited for all it is worth. People who spend a few hours at a local beauty spot do not usually spend much money; those who settle for two weeks in a particular area are contributing significantly to the local economy, but they will only come if there is enough to keep them interested throughout their holiday. The scenery may be splendid, but you cannot see it in the dark, and sitting in a hotel room watching television is less comfortable than doing it at home, while the countryside, be it ever so beautiful, does lose some of its charm in a heavy downpour. Evening and indoor entertainment needs to be provided, too, and what can be used by visitors will also be available to residents. In this connection, the disdain for caravan sites is also misplaced. Properly stocked village shops can benefit enormously from their trade, and again what is good for the tourist is good for the local. Care obviously must be taken over their positioning: too often in the past they have been eyesores, but a properly landscaped, wooded site with a high standard of facilities – restaurant, bar, showers, games room, perhaps even a miniature golf course – could be an asset to a rural area deprived of jobs and income.

None of these necessary changes in attitude will occur by itself, or under the present unsatisfactory and rather shamefaced way in which tourism is approached at government level. If, as official pronouncements maintain, tourism is to become an important feature of our economic performance, with particular reference to the countryside, then the government should put its money where its mouth is and establish a ministry of tourism, as other much-visited countries have done, to determine and organize policy and supervise the way in which it is carried out. One important function of this ministry would be to analyse demand and identify trends, so that facilities could be offered that were not entirely dependent on the whims of fickle fashion. How much time, for example, do foreign visitors spend in towns and cities as compared with the countryside? When they do visit rural areas, what are they looking for? Are there ways of spreading the burden of visitors so that more areas of the countryside will benefit from the income? We know which the most popular regions are, but what attractions can be offered in less well-known areas? It is no good simply sticking a label saying Area of Outstanding Natural Beauty on a bit of countryside: what makes it outstanding should be described in detail and ways of making it attractive from other points of view should be exploited. The British climate is too temperate to be of much use as a tourist attraction, but seasonal attractions could be investigated. Some parts of the country are at their best in spring, others in winter, and so on.

Working with the ministry would be regional tourism departments, not only to promote the specific appeal of their areas but also to manage the effects of tourism on them and their populations. The whole of the countryside cannot be thrown open to visitors, any more than to ramblers, and while tourists cannot be herded into particular places and utterly excluded from others, a degree of direction can be achieved by managing the availability of amenities, accommodation, transport and other things. Tourist areas need an off-season to allow them to recover. In spite of what some environmentalists seem to believe, there has never been a time when mankind has not exploited its surroundings to their contemporary limits, and often beyond. One of the good things achieved by environmentalist concern has been the identification of our contemporary limits and, thanks to scientific advances, some of the future ones, too. But that does not mean we should be looking back to older, allegedly kinder methods of exploitation, or to stop it altogether. In the modern context, tourism can be an acceptable and, if properly organized, a relatively kind way of making our surroundings work for us, bearing in mind that if the countryside is not generally seen to have some useful function it will ultimately be discarded. Mass interest in matters rural, particularly among city-dwellers, is a fairly recent phenomenon and for the present remains novel. We cannot know when some other novelty will appear to supersede it.

It must be stressed, however, that the promotion of tourism and leisure activities in general provide by no means the only answer to the question of what we should do with the large areas of countryside that will be left more or less without an occupation as a result of the coming contraction in agriculture. The belief of some sections of the heritage industry, that if we have nothing to offer of the present we can make up for it by selling the past or the scenery, is wrong. A countryside constructed according to the images of tourist brochures would be as lifeless in human terms as one handed over to the conservationists, and would decay just as surely, producing the sort of scenes imagined by some futurist writers who have forecast huge, high-tech cities surrounded by wilderness in which only the dispossessed and the despairing make their primitive homes. Early signs of what could happen may be discerned in some of the more popular areas for holiday cottages, with an average of one house in five occupied for only a few months of each year and in a few particular villages – in Cornwall and North Wales, for instance – 50 per cent of the properties owned by people who live elsewhere.

The holiday cottage, whatever its owner might think, is really no more than a form of tourism, and as such it requires regulation. There are no methods available in a democratic society for preventing people from buying second homes; that would require a degree of central control over where people might live more appropriate to a paranoid totalitarian regime. Furthermore, contrary to what some Welsh arsonists might think, there is nothing morally wrong with possessing two houses. That said, however, there is nothing very attractive in the prospect of a wintry countryside dotted with dark, deserted villages, and holiday homes are of more economic benefit to their owners than to the areas in which they are situated. Taxes such as that levied in the Irish Republic on second homes may act as a discouragement in some cases, but there will always be people willing and able to pay them, and in any case it must be better that a country cottage is occupied some of the time rather than not at all. Once more, it is a matter of a positive rather than a negative attitude, and there are means by which the craze for second homes could be exploited to the general good.

For a start, planning restrictions could be revised in certain areas to allow the construction of houses specifically designed for weekenders and holidaymakers. Time-share arrangements have already begun to attract people to some areas of Britain, and on a carefully controlled scale this development could be extended to embrace full ownership. The huge developments for 5000 people to which I referred in Chapter Five would almost certainly be unwelcome and inappropriate, and one can only applaud the decision of the Department of the Environment to reject a proposal for a relatively small complex of that type at White Cross Bay on Lake Windermere. There are already enough problems with mass tourism in the most appreciated areas of the countryside without adding further pressure in the form of mass holiday accommodation. That said, however, the tendency to resist any sort of tourist facilities in 'beauty spots' must be tempered by common sense and some regard for the wider community. The solution is not to ban everything, but to permit only small, selected and compatible developments that would help to spread demand over a wider area, rather than concentrating it in a few popular places, as tends to happen at present. Existing holiday cottages could be converted into more of a local asset by offering incentives to owners to let them to other holidaymakers for a prescribed number of weeks each year, thus helping to attract visitors and income to the area. At another level, rural communities could have some control over the numbers of holiday homes in their areas through a simple requirement that when a cottage came on the market it must be offered first to the local authority, perhaps at a fair market price to be determined by the district valuer. Such properties could be bought by the authority itself for letting, or made available for assisted purchase by people on housing waiting lists. Alternatively, a notice of sale could be sent to every resident of the district so that all had the opportunity of buying, and if no local need was identified, the cottage could be sold on the open market, second home or not.

Tourism in whatever form, from ramblers and day-trippers to country-house hotels and holiday cottages, is a factor to be reckoned with in the present state of the countryside and in its future. Like agriculture, development, commuters and conservation, mass tourism presents a challenge with the potential to enhance or damage the fabric of rural existence. It is how we respond to that series of challenges, how we recognize and manage the irresistible pressure for change, that will determine the rural heritage we pass on to our descendants, not how many woods and fields and 'traditional' villages we preserve in the state in which we found them.

SEVEN

A Country Living

Nor rural sights alone, but rural sounds,
Exhilarate the spirit, and restore
The tone of languid Nature

William Cowper, *The Task*

By 1989 it had become apparent that in Britain growing and multiplying pressure groups dedicated to the environment, conservation, wildlife and the countryside had replaced the trade unions as the most powerful extra-parliamentary political force, in terms of both membership and financial support. Applications to join the most prominent organizations such as Greenpeace, Friends of the Earth, the National Trust, the Council for the Protection of Rural England and so on were running at, on average, about 3000 a week and several opinion polls identified environmental issues as being very high, and rising, on the list of public concerns. To emphasize the strength of this movement, the Green Party appeared from nowhere to win 15 per cent of the British vote in elections to the European Parliament, devastating the parties of the centre-left and almost catching up with Labour in the South-East with a score of 20.3 per cent and in the South-West with 19.6 per cent. Because of Britain's first-past-the-post electoral system, the Greens won no seats in Europe, and given that their vote in the 1987 national election was just 89,000, the two main political parties seemed to have little to fear in parliamentary terms for the immediate future; but it was clear that they could no longer ignore the potential strength of the environmentalist lobby.

One reason for this was its range. Analysis of the voting in the European election provided convincing evidence that many of those who supported the Greens in Britain were by no means their natural allies. Indeed significant numbers, it appeared, were unfamiliar with the finer points of Green politics, which in broad terms are diametrically opposed to the ideas of consumption, competition, freer trade and economic growth which had been election-winners for the Conservative Party for more than a decade and elements of which had even begun to change the policies of the Labour Party. What appealed even to people who would be horrified at the prospect of heavy taxes on imports and exports, the abolition of commercial banks, lower standards of living and a publicly funded salary for everyone, working or not, was simply the environmental and conservation content of the Green approach.

Now it cannot be denied that there are definite attractions in the Greens' ecological views: the world has reached – perhaps long passed – a stage of development when it needs to consider how to treat itself more kindly in the future. Matters such as the depletion of the ozone layer and the prospect of global warming exacerbated by the excessive use of fossil fuels cannot be ignored; and as is demonstrated by the generally tardy and rather half-hearted progress made in the introduction and use of lead-free petrol, not to mention the feeble efforts to produce renewable sources of energy, business and government cannot be left to themselves in the pious hope that they will see sense one day. Changes that upset long-established habits, beliefs and practices, which have survived because they are easy and profitable, have to be forced. The old ways, no matter how dangerous, are nevertheless safer for those who have grown rich on them, or those who find them convenient. That the Greens should fix these problems in the public attention, and campaign for change, is a good thing. It is in their solutions where questions begin to arise.

Green ideology is unashamedly fundamentalist and, like religious fundamentalism, it suffers from a number of serious defects. For one thing, it begins with the belief that civilization has deviated from the path of righteousness, as if that had been set at some time in the distant past and there had been a choice between the 'good' way and the 'bad'. The truth is, of course, that development, either human or physical, does not move in straight lines, so that there is not one simple choice, but myriad choices, each of which carries advantages and disadvantages, benefits and losses. Sometimes, indeed, there is no choice at all – movement is involuntary and occasioned by chance. Coal was not invented by some mad scientist intent on destroying the world; it was handed to us by nature and we accidentally discovered that it would burn, with consequences that have been immeasurably beneficial but can now be seen to be in some ways measurably harmful. That does not mean we should or even can go back and start again, as if the properties of coal had never been appreciated and exploited. History will not go into reverse. What it does mean is that the benefits of coal have helped us to reach a stage where we can see the disadvantages and thus have now given us a choice: does that make coal 'good' or 'bad'?

The absolute distinction between good and bad, right and wrong, is another disturbing feature of fundamentalist thinking, along with the presumption that the so-called bad and wrong must simply be excised. In the Green vocabulary, nuclear power is bad and wrong and the answer is to stop it, to pretend it never happened and to rely instead on things that are considered good and right. Only a fool would deny that there are terrifying dangers associated with nuclear power, but only a fundamentalist would refuse to see that its benefits offer a more optimistic assessment, which is that we should devote every effort towards controlling and harnessing nuclear energy until its risks have been removed or at least reduced to a negligible level. Fundamentalism also suffers from an inability to see the future outside the framework of the past, believing not that we should go boldly forward but that we should either remain timidly where we are or even retreat ignominiously to where we were. It is a central feature of Green thinking that we have gone just about as far as we can go, that if we do not stop now we will destroy ourselves and the planet – a modern version of the man with the placard saying 'Repent, for the End of the World is Nigh'. If we had all believed the man with the placard, his prediction would have been self-fulfilling.

Yet it is the pessimistic, fundamentalist view that, for the moment, appears to have captured what politicians like to call the moral high ground. In some ways, that is healthy, as I suggested earlier. Increased public awareness of environmental issues is no bad thing, and pressure from consumers for manufacturers to control pollution and to develop products that are less wasteful and less dangerous can only result in benefits for everyone. The risk is that awareness soon becomes anxiety, which in turn can so easily develop into panic, especially when it is whipped up by propaganda and a popular press that reduces thoughts to slogans and exaggerates rumour into fact. A rapid progression of that sort occurred when proper concern over what appeared to be relatively rare occurrences of food poisoning exploded into mass hysteria that not only made Britons look ridiculous in the eyes of the rest of the world but also cost them a great deal of money as the government used public funds to bail out the egg and poultry industry, devastated by ill-founded accusations that it was the cause of what by then had been blown up into an epidemic of salmonella.

So far as the countryside is concerned, such an atmosphere of pessimism and panic is now firmly entrenched, and growing more widespread as individuals, politicians and commercial interests jostle to leap on to that part of the Green bandwagon that suits their purposes and to outdo each other in establishing what are thought to be environmentalist credentials. In such circumstances, it is becoming more difficult for the voice of common sense to be heard, to separate the facts from the fundamentalist fancies and to prevent the fanatics from leading us into reactions and decisions that we may come to regret. It is now almost impossible for new housing development to be mentioned without the addition of the adjectives 'ugly' and 'characterless', or to speak of change in rural areas without using terms such as 'ruin' or 'destruction' or 'despoliation'. Everything possible is being done to express rejection of the new in favour of the old, to resist regeneration in favour of stagnation. The general impression being fostered by conservationists, environmentalists and the heritage industry is that those parts of the countryside that are not being turned into vast housing estates are on the point of becoming poisoned, polluted wastelands.

In the spring of 1989, the formation of yet another conservationist/heritage pressure group was mooted, with the faintly ludicrous title of The Smaller Historic Towns and Villages Association and the aim of preventing developers from 'turning many of the country's most distinctive and beautiful villages into characterless estates' and 'ruining' their communities. Just why a community should be ruined rather than invigorated by the addition of new members was not explained by the founders of the new organization, whose primary complaint appeared to be that their smaller historic towns and villages did not look the same as they had done when they were mentioned in the Domesday Book. (No doubt The Smaller Historic Towns and Villages Association will soon be followed by The Society of Tiny Historic Villages and Hamlets.) The protesters were reported as believing that 'the towns and villages have lost their character because councils and successive governments have moved away from controlling the design and colour of buildings and because many authorities have failed to produce comprehensive district plans to control development.' In Tenterden, Kent, for example, the provision of a new leisure centre at a cost of £4 million caused outrage because the building was 'futuristic' – one of the most damning descriptions in conservationspeak. Yet if we are building for the future, where is the rationale for doing it in the style of the past? In looking forward, we do not deny what has gone before: let us by all means preserve the Norman churches and the quaint old cottages, but let us not fall into the trap of believing that we are unfit to do anything but continue reproducing them ad infinitum.

The Prince of Wales added to the assumption of the unworthiness of modern man by criticizing builders for what was seen as 'failing' to use traditional regional materials and designs. It is surely an odd view of the world that sees technical progress as failure. It is even odder that one so interested in the conservation of the countryside should be advocating the use of materials – presumably such as stone and wood – the provision of which would require even larger-scale deforestation and the development of more quarries to 'scar the landscape'.

We are entering the realms of fantasy here. The population of England in the late Middle Ages was 4.1 million, of which only a fraction could afford proper housing anyway, and by the golden age of English ruralism it had increased to just 6.5 million. In Britain today we require housing for nearly 57 million people, of whom 20 per cent live in rural areas. Consider how many tons of stone and reeds would be required to house 11.5 million people in charming thatched cottages. The prevailing *Wind in the Willows* mentality simply ignores the facts that do not suit its Elysian imagination: 'traditional' materials could not cope with our needs, and even if they could the costs would be prohibitive. It is sometimes hard to resist the conclusion that rural traditionalists wish to control not only the appearance of new housing but also the type of people who occupy it.

The question of the design of new housing is more complicated because it is entirely subjective. Presumably people do not, unless they are quite desperate, burden themselves with a lifetime of debt in order to live in a modern bungalow which they actively dislike. Presumably, too, architects do not set out to design buildings notable principally for their ugliness. Unfortunately, cost is the overwhelming consideration in most private housing today, and therefore one of the chief reasons for the appearance of the developments so detested by the traditionalists. What the 'charm school' does not appear to realize, however, is that its own opposition contributes greatly to the very thing it opposes. As the House Builders Federation has pointed out, the presumption of planning policies against development artificially restricts the supply of land available for building and inflates its price, so that both profitability and affordability depend more than is necessary on density, which naturally affects design. Tighter planning laws of the sort for which so many conservationists campaign will only serve to make matters worse. What we need are regulations that release more land for development, and work in its favour, while at the same time providing strict guidelines for the types and numbers of houses that can be built in specific locations.

On the East Coast of the United States, for instance, where history is guarded almost as jealously as in England, zoning policies are often based on the permitted sizes of building plots – it might be a quarter of an acre or less in urban areas, rising to one acre in suburbs and two acres in rural districts. Thus one village where I lived in Massachusetts had grown from a tiny colonial settlement into a pleasing mixture of houses ranging from carefully preserved seventeenth-century farms through a variety of styles (both genuine and copied) to strikingly futuristic and energy-efficient constructions in brick and glass. Local planning officials had understood that the way to preserve both character and a thriving, harmonious community was not simply to stop what might be considered inferior design but to create conditions in which good design could flourish. It is worth remarking that in spite of a relatively high concentration of people and the presence of every modern amenity, from leisure centre to vast supermarket, that village was one of the most pleasant and tranquil places in which I have ever lived.

There is, too, a more general point to be made about the design of housing, which is that there is always a gap between the development of styles and the public perception. Generally people prefer the familiar because they have learnt to understand it, and this very acquaintance tends to distort their appreciation of something new. If the 'character' of a village is fixed by what is already there, it follows that any addition is going to cause confusion until it in turn becomes familiar: what is really objected to is not the building itself, but the interruption of intimacy it represents. Objectively speaking, there is nothing particularly offensive in the modern bungalows about which some residents of places such as Downham Market, in Norfolk, have worked themselves into a frenzy. The bungalow, after all, might be said to be the twentieth-century equivalent of the standard country cottage of earlier times – small, unassuming and cosy. What can be irritating is simply the visual disturbance to a previously known landscape, but that, of course, will disappear through time, unless resentment against it is nursed. Many of the rural buildings now valued so highly would have caused similar disturbance, and given rise to similar resentment, when they were first constructed, because for most people acceptance of something new can never be on its own terms, but only through their knowledge of the old.

Sadly, there is at present no sign that the accelerated pace of development in modern times – that is, the more rapid and widespread appearance of new things – has contributed to a more positive attitude towards its acceptance, and certainly not in the countryside. Rather the reverse, if anything. Thus in 1989 the Countryside Commission, which ought to be more thoughtful about such things, was arguing against not only housing estates round villages ('bland and suburban-looking' and 'ill-adapted' to their surroundings), but also against the construction of what it called isolated housing in rural areas, on the ground that 'no form of development would more rapidly destroy the essential character of the countryside and impoverish landscape diversity'. Apart from the fact that such an attitude does not appear to leave much room for worthwhile development at all, it fails to take account of some important factors. In the past, most rural housing for ordinary people was not designed to fit in with the landscape: its appearance was conditioned by much the same things that obtain today, cost, demand and the availability of materials. The only reason why old villages appear to be adapted to their surroundings is because that is where they are.

Then, as I have already said, the Commission's expressed concern about suggestions that planning controls might be relaxed makes high-density housing more rather than less likely in areas where building does take place. If it is genuinely interested, as it claims, in a planning system that achieves 'a better balance between people and their environment', the Commission should be campaigning for more land to be released for construction, with appropriate controls, so that plot prices are reduced and more of the cost-content of new housing arises from design and technical features. That is the way to prevent 'bland' and 'characterless' building and to stop villages being swamped by large estates.

As for 'isolated housing', it might be argued that such developments may add to the diversity of landscape, rather than diminishing it. After all, if the construction of isolated housing had been prohibited in the past, we would now be lacking a substantial number of smaller historic villages and hamlets to protect. Above all, however, the scale of what the Countryside Commission and others see as the destruction of the countryside must be borne in mind. In England and Wales during 1988, the *total* number of new permanent dwellings completed – urban and rural – was 195,764 and the amount of rural land of which the nation was deprived was just 12,000 acres. That is a ratio of one new house for every 59 people who already live in the countryside and one acre for every 950 rural dwellers. What we are seeing, it seems, in all the protests and hand-wringing, is nothing more than a self-righteous justification of the Nimby syndrome: let there be development, but let it be somewhere other than where the traditionalists can see it.

One unwelcome effect of the atmosphere of impending doom generated by the anti-development lobby has been actually to increase the demand for living space in the countryside, a sort of 'buy now while stocks last' approach. In public opinion polls, about 80 per cent of those questioned said they would prefer to live in the country. What most meant, however, was that they wanted rural living and urban work, the worst possible type of development for the countryside. Regrettably, the pattern emerging in the late 1980s confirmed that trend. Commercial enterprises moving out of London, or planning to in the near future, were settling on a ring of towns within about seventy miles of the capital. Cambridge, Swindon and Peterborough had been popular relocation targets for some years, but their very popularity had prompted cost-cutting companies to look elsewhere, so that towns such as Corby, Banbury and Northampton had been 'discovered'. With some 10,000 jobs set to move out of London in 1990, more small, free-standing towns were likely to be selected, most probably in the East Midlands, partly because the region is less crowded than the old industrial areas of the West Midlands and partly because continuing electrification of railways would allow rapid access to London when necessary.

Some of the workers thus relocated will obviously want to live in the towns selected by their employers, but many are likely to seize the chance of realizing the popular dream of the rural idyll (especially in view of the growing social problems evident in enlarged provincial towns, to which I referred earlier), and will look for property in nearby villages, thus spreading the effects already seen in the South-East and East Anglia and consolidating the network of suburbanization that has been spreading out from London.

It was predicted that such development would not spread north of the River Humber, where 'real' countryside is to be found. The prospect of the North–South divide remained, but in an interesting new form, with the rural areas of the South becoming increasingly suburban and those of the North continuing to be depopulated of natives in search of work – as has been the trend in recent years – and left partly as empty landscape in the hands of the conservationists and partly as rich pickings for prosperous southern executives in search of holiday cottages. In both those trends, it is not difficult to discern the makings of a wasteland of the future. If that ever comes about, it will be the result not of planning controls that were too slack, but of regulations that were too tight and applied too rigidly in the wrong way, and of misdirected efforts to 'save' the landscape and 'protect our rural heritage'. To prevent the suburbanization of countryside in some areas while others are gradually abandoned for the purposes of normal living, we should be thinking about limiting development in small provincial towns within easy reach of London and directing it towards more rural areas, particularly those in the North, Yorkshire and Humberside, the West Midlands, the North-West and Scotland, where outward migration has been most marked. Yes, some countryside would be 'lost', but probably less, and more evenly distributed, than will be the case with the creeping expansion in the South-East that current policies encourage.

Such a change, of course, would imply serious improvement of communications, particularly roads in regions that are not well served at present. Unfortunately, the conservation lobby is opposed to that, too. It has long been realized that the east coast lacks a proper trunk route, that the M1 is seriously overcrowded and the A1 is a joke. Proposals to remedy this by extending the M11 northwards over the Humber bridge, however, produced an outcry from the likes of the Ramblers Association, which flatly condemned the plan as 'an environmental catastrophe' for the North York Moors National Park. 'Any road across the park would seriously harm its superb coastline, or cut a deep chasm through the moor.' The preferred solution was that 'the route must run to the west of the park, along existing transport corridors in the Vale of York'. In other words, let us funnel even more traffic into a system that is already inadequate, through areas which are relatively populated, rather than providing environmental relief with a new road that would interfere with the lives of fewer people. Once more the rationale is as incomprehensible as it is indefatigable.

Why should it be so? Why must we cling grimly to what we have at all costs, even that of denying ourselves what we might have in the future? At the end of the revolutionary 1960s, in an article entitled 'The Myth of England', John Holloway identified history as the root of many of the nation's weaknesses. 'There was just too much English history,' he wrote. 'Too much had happened, too many different and contrasting things had happened, too much could be made of it, too many ways.' In the reactionary 1980s we can see what he meant. A growing obsession with our history, in all its variegated forms, embracing all its inconsistencies as if they were part of the same whole, celebrating all its self-created and mutually opposing legends, has made us not only fear the future but also reject the present. If we do not recognize and respond to the way we are now, instead of always wishing ourselves back into earlier times, there is a strong possibility that our past is all we shall be left with, and we shall be forced into realizing how uncomfortable it was.

I try to remain optimistic, but at the time of writing there is no sign that any significant change of attitude is likely or that anyone has a realistic vision of a future for the countryside. As we have seen, one of the most crucial decisions to be taken is that concerning agricultural policy. It is a decision that continues to be avoided. In 1989 the European Community was congratulating itself on its quota and price-cutting systems in reducing food surpluses, notwithstanding the fact that removing the butter mountain and the milk lake had actually cost it an additional £6000 million in two years. Nor was the reduction of stocks an overall one. As the surpluses of dairy products and wheat dwindled, those of beef and barley remained almost unchanged, while intervention stocks of durum wheat and rye rose slightly, that of olive oil almost doubled, and a surplus of 185,000 tonnes of oil seeds appeared within twelve months. And while subsidies in the form of price guarantees were being restricted to a rise of 1.9 per cent a year until

1992, the Community was gaily offering farmers new subsidies of as much as £200 a hectare to stop farming on at least 20 per cent of their land for five years. In other words, if the subsidies produce unforeseen and unwelcome results, subsidize them out of existence. Heaven forbid that we should admit we were wrong, analyse our mistakes and arrive at some new ideas.

The British government, meanwhile, went one better in the name of environmental protection. While announcing that spending on agricultural commodities would fall by a very substantial amount in 1989, it promptly offered to give farmers back almost half a million pounds in payments for 'environmentally sensitive' management of land which they had already been paid to set aside. Starting with the counties of Bedfordshire, Cambridgeshire, Essex, Hertfordshire, Norfolk, Northamptonshire and Suffolk, farmers could be eligible for:

£45 a hectare for providing habitats on light, well-drained soils for stone curlews, lapwings and other ground-nesting birds;

£85 a hectare for planting shrubs, broadleaved trees and hedgerows on the margins of fallow fields;

£90 a hectare for providing grassland within three miles of coasts that could be used for winter grazing by Brent geese;

£120 a hectare for providing new meadows for the benefit of wildlife and 'the quiet enjoyment' of the public.

It might perhaps be wondered if anyone noticed the irony of introducing such a scheme during what had been designated British Food and Farming Year. Food and farming are the last things the new payments are designed to encourage. Rather, as well as being an expensive means of cutting back on production, such subsidies are a way of attempting to move little bits of countryside back a generation or two, to assuage the strange sense of guilt we have acquired as a result of our success in leaving the past behind.

But the idea of turning farmers into park-keepers began to look like nothing more than a harmless joke beside another, more

sinister manifestation of an environmentalist ethic that is becoming
ever more confident of the rightness of its cause, and arrogant in
the pursuit of it. In Wales, about a thousand acres of trees were
burned down in six separate fires. The fires were started deliberately; the trees, of course, were conifers. An organization calling
itself Ashes wrote to a Welsh newspaper:

> Our beautiful country has been blighted by the indiscriminate
> planting done by the Forestry Commission. These are the
> latest of many planned fires. It is our intention to rid the whole
> of Great Britain of this type of action by the Forestry
> Commission.

The most disturbing factor of the fundamentalism I mentioned
earlier is its tendency to attract the fanatic and, clearly, the lunatic.
Conservationists have condemned the vicious activities of Ashes,
but they, and their assorted allies of ecologists, environmentalists,
traditionalists, ramblers and the whole panoply of the countryside
lobby, have only themselves to blame, for the self-righteousness
of their tone and the casual violence of their language.

The resolution of complex issues can assume a simplicity that is
positively frightening with the conviction of one's rightness and
even more so with the belief that one is acting out of selfless
concern. The fur trade is cruel: fire-bomb the shops that sell furs.
The use of animals in scientific experiments is morally wrong: break
up the laboratories. Holiday cottages and incomers are an affront
to national pride: set fire to their houses. Conifers are alien: burn
them. The latest gang of arsonists are like their predecessors in that
they operate on a system of logic that feeds only on itself. No
matter that the Forestry Commission has begun to respond to the
complaints, reducing the size of new plantations, increasing the
proportion of deciduous trees solely for landscape enhancement,
planning eight new forest nature reserves in Wales, covering 3000
acres. No matter that wood imports cost Britain well over a billion
pounds a year, and rising. No matter that 6000 people in Wales
depend on the forestry and timber industry for their livelihood, and
that the figure is likely soon to approach 10,000. All that matters is

the single, blinkered vision nursed by criminally-minded fantasists at odds with the real world that surrounds them.

It is this sort of absolutism, though fortunately in a less violent form, for the present at least, which substitutes for any sort of policy that would make sense of the countryside, that would determine how best we might use it, what the real needs of its residents are and how far it should be viewed as a leisure resource in the light of the other resources it offers. The conservationists and the environmentalists are perhaps the people most aware of the problems – or some of them, anyway – but that does not mean they are the only source of solutions, because their priorities may conflict with others that do not interest them, because they have in general only one point of view. A distinction must be made between claims for preservation that identify a genuine case, in the interests of both countryside and society in general, and those that, at bottom, are no more than an example of the very selfishness with which the conservation/environmental/heritage lobby is so fond of charging those whose views differ from its own conventional wisdom.

The pressure for change in the countryside is evident. Even if only 10 per cent of the people who say they would prefer rural life have the opportunity to achieve their ambition, that means finding room among the green fields for an additional four-and-a-half million inhabitants or a rise in the rural population of more than 30 per cent. As I have already pointed out, the romance of ruralism has long been a potent force in British society. It is even reflected in the names people give their houses. 'The Cottage' and 'Rose Cottage' came second and third in a popularity poll conducted by the Halifax Building Society among its fifteen million investors and borrowers. (The most popular appellation, 'The Bungalow', is perhaps rather neutral, but the fact that people name their houses at all suggests leanings towards places where the houses are not grouped in streets.) The romance has been intensified by the activities of the countryside lobby, to the extent that 'country parks' have now begun to appear in cities for the benefit of those who cannot otherwise enjoy the perceived privileges of rural life. The lobby cannot complain, and in truth is in no position to resist, when large numbers of people decide to claim what is constantly being identified for them as their inheritance.

Meanwhile, the countryside is losing some of its raison d'être as agriculture is forced by changing circumstances and political incompetence into decline in terms of both food production and employment. Do we seriously want large parts of it to return to the wild, its only purpose to support flora and fauna and to provide quiet enjoyment, or could we use some newly available land wisely and beneficially for more tangible human or economic needs, to replace those which have sustained it thus far? And what of the rural population that does not share the privileges of the new squirearchy, the poor, the ill-housed, the deprived, the unemployed? The countryside should be used to help them, too.

What is required now is some serious reflection and, above all, a greater degree of moderation. The pressure groups have made their point. The countryside is precious and must not be wasted. But if that is so, it is too precious to be a battleground, for that more than anything will ensure that it is wasted. We must recognize that the questions are not simple and the answers are even harder, that they involve not only the past but also the future, not only possible loss but also possible gain. We must listen to the voices of those whose interest in the countryside, while encompassing hedgerows and meadows, wildflowers and Brent geese, moorlands and mountains, actually ranges rather more widely, those for whom a country living includes people. We must remember that green is not a primary colour: it can be produced by mixing, and it comes in a great variety of shades.

FURTHER READING

Burton, Anthony, and May, John, *Landscape Detective*, Allen & Unwin, 1986

Coones, Paul, and Patten, John, *The Penguin Guide to the Landscape of England and Wales*, Penguin Books, 1986

Drewett, Peter; Rudling, David; Gardiner, Mark, *The South-East to AD 1000*, Longman, 1988

Haggard, H. Rider, *A Farmer's Year*, The Cresset Library, 1987

Hewison, Robert, *The Heritage Industry*, Methuen, 1987

Howitt, William, *The Rural Life of England* (3rd edition), Irish University Press, Dublin, 1971

Marwick, Arthur, *British Society since 1945*, Pelican, 1988

Mingay, G. E., *The Transformation of Britain 1830–1939*, Paladin, 1987

Newby, Howard, *The Countryside in Question*, Hutchinson, 1988

Rich, Lawrence, *Inherit the Land*, Unwin Hyman, 1987

Shoard, Marion, *This Land is Our Land*, Paladin, 1987

Sutherland, Douglas, *The Landowners*, Frederick Muller, 1988

Wood, Michael, *Domesday: A Search for the Roots of England*, BBC Publications, 1986

PHOTO CREDITS

INDEX

Agricultural and Food Research Council
  38, 52
  genetic engineering crop research 39,
  52
  on 'biological research' in farming 37
Anti-Corn Law League 3
Apples 39
Areas of Outstanding Natural Beauty
  (AONBs) 21, 102, 104, 105, 128,
  129
Ashbrook, Kate 157
Ashes organization 189
Association of District Councils 71
  The Future for Rural Communities,
  1988 125

Baker, Kenneth 129, 130
Banbury: relocation target for industry
  from London 185
Barber, Sir Derek 95
Bedford Level, East Anglia: unsound
  drainage scheme 14
Ben Wyvis, Scotland: opposition to ski
  development at 164
Berthon, Sir Stephen 108
Brecon Beacons National Park 95
British Equestrian Trade Association 161
British Field Sports Society 161, 162
British Food and Farming Year, 1989
  188
British landscape development 7
  Bronze Age 8

destruction of virgin forest 11
doubling of built-up area, 1900–50
  16–17
enclosures 12
farming becomes a business 12–13
hunting land 12
Iron Age 8
medieval 12
need for conservation and development
  25, 26
Norman 10–11
Roman 8–9
romantic view of countryside after
  Industrial Revolution 15–16
rural poverty 15, 16
Saxon 9–10
Stone Age 7–8
'traditional' landscape 6–7, 76
Victorian 77
work of 'Improvers' 13, 14
British Tourist Authority 165
British Trust for Conservation Volunteers
  104
Broads, the 96

California: replacement of redwood
  forests 112
Cambridge: relocation target for industry
  from London 185
Cannock Chase 153
Central Statistical Office 123
Cereals: as sources of chemicals 39

Channel Tunnel: preservation of displaced plant life 112
Charles, Prince of Wales 37, 181
Chatsworth: number of yearly visitors 152
Church of England Commission for Rural Areas 73
Clayton, Michael 161
Colton, Charles Caleb: *Lacon* 61
Common Agricultural Policy (CAP) 30–1, 57
  costs 32
  farming subsidies and grants 42, 44, 45
  fraud in 32
  surpluses 32, 187
Confederation of British Industry (CBI) 131
Conservation 89–90
  anthropomorphism in 91
  best environment equated with late nineteenth century 92–3
  biological restoration 111–14
  bodies concerned with 104
  confusion in 104–5
  conservationists' inconsistency 91–2
  doubts about 'blanket' protection of landscape 109
  efficient 106–7
  example of conflict with rural life 107–9
  increase of urban strain via 128
  wrongly equated with 'preservation' 90, 180
Conservative Party 178
  Conference, 1988 118
  problems with conservation v. business 23
  renewed interest in countryside 5
Coones, Paul and Patten, John
  on concept of English village 11
  on rural houses of poor 14, 15
  Penguin Guide to the Landscape of England and Wales 11, 12
Corby: relocation target for industry from London 185
Costa Rica: replacement of dry-forest 112
Council for National Parks 104

Council for the Protection of Rural England 104
  condemns farming methods 36
  deplores over-popularity of Ilkley Moor 152, 163
  recommends old-fashioned farming 42–3
Country Homes and Interiors 152, 159
Country Life 68
Country towns
  acquire problems of larger towns 134–6
  need for controlled development 138–9
Countryside, British
  changes in traditions 76–7
  controversy over 3–4
  'country habit' 5, 26
  creating non-agricultural employment base 80–4
  desire to prevent change 17, 21–2, 26
  dilemma of public access and spoliation 153, 159–60
  errors of rural protectionists 17–21
  merging of urban and rural property markets 78–9
  merit of conservationist case 24
  'our heritage' view 6, 18, 40
  over-protection by environmentalists 20, 21–2
  poverty today 117
  problem of decaying local property 75
  property boom 78–80
  restrictions on building 119–25
  self-sufficiency of country people 66–7
  suitable construction in 111
  tourism, *see* separate entry
  transfer of farmland to urban uses, 1950s–80s 119
  work of development agencies 130–1
  See also British landscape development and Ruralism
Countryside Commission 95, 96, 99, 100, 101, 104, 107, 109
  argues against rural housing development 184
Countryside Review Committee 41, 46, 76, 90, 105, 110, 151

Conservation and the Countryside Heritage 89
Leisure and the Countryside 160
on approach to rural problems 82–3
Cowper, William: *The Task* 177
CRACK (Campaign for River Access for Canoes and Kayaks) 158

Dartmoor National Park 94–5, 97–8
Department of the Environment 56, 96, 126, 134, 142, 143, 172
on employment in rural areas 118–19
on Green Belts 127
problems with planning restrictions and reviving rural economy 23–4, 122, 140
Development Commission 139
employment programmes for countryside, 1985 130
Devonshire, Duke of 152
Domesday Book 10, 11, 181
Dower, John 93
Dyfed: large elderly population 64

East Anglia
artifically created shortage of building land 121
cheaper housing than London's, 1986 63
drift from towns to, 1980s 61, 121
large elderly population 13
lower than average crime rate 63
rise in cost of building land 69
rise in house prices, 1987 69
Economic Forestry group 156
Economist, The 34, 40
criticises EEC 41
criticises Ministry of Agriculture 33
on reality of modern life 19
Edinburgh, Duke of: Inquiry into British Housing, 1985 119
Egg and poultry industry: food poisoning scare 180
English Heritage 104
prosecutes Marquis of Hertford 20
Enlightenment, the 13

Environmentally Sensitive Areas (ESAs) 43, 104, 105, 107
European Community 4, 53, 101
cost of reducing food surpluses 187
subsidies to farmers to stop farming 188
See also Common Agricultural Policy
Evening Standard: attacks tax concessions for conifer planting 49–50

Farming in Britain
area of farmland 29
condemnation of modern methods 35–8
decline in number of farms and workers 54
diversification 46, 53
drop in incomes, 1980s 45
effect of EC on 30–2
exposed to market forces, 1980s 34–5
Farm Woodland Scheme 46, 47, 51, 52
government subsidies for 'environmentally sensitive' land management 188
'greenhouse effect' and 40
heavy borrowing by farmers 45
high production 29–30
inter-war depression 34–5
limits on production, 1980s 33, 41–2
lost potential for employment 24
Milk Outgoers Scheme 42
need for housing on surplus land 55–6, 136–7
need for less government interference 56–7
need to discourage farming in marginal areas 44, 45, 54–5
number of farms 29
organic farming 35, 37–8, 43
paying farmers not to produce 42, 43, 44, 188
percentage of rural employment in 54
portrayal of farmers as villains 33, 34
proposal for production entitlement guarantees 57–8
relations with government 30, 33–4, 35, 41

Farming in Britain *cont.*
  research 38–9, 52
  surpluses 31, 32, 33
Flax, 39
Food industry in Britain 38
Forestry Commission 47, 51, 52, 94,
  156, 189
  plantations in West Wales 49
Forestry in Britain 46–52
  conservationists' opposition to conifers
    48–9
  Farm Woodland Scheme 46, 47, 51, 52
  forest area, 1987 47
  hardwoods and softwoods 48, 51–2
  planting grants 51
  private commercial woodland 47
  Scottish 133
  tax concessions for investors 47, 49,
    133
Fosse Way 8–9
Fountain Forestry company: outcry over
  tree-planting in Flow Country 50–1,
  133
Foxhunting 160–3
Friends of the Earth 36, 50, 177

Goldsmith, Oliver 13, 14
Gray, Thomas 13
  Elegy 83, 85
Great Outdoors, The (magazine) 159
Green Belts 119–22 *passim*, 126, 129,
  137, 140
  purpose behind 127, 130
  rural dream in creation of 128
Green Party: success in European election
  177
Greene, Henry 112
'Greenhouse effect' 40, 178
Greenpeace 177
Greens, the
  ecological views 178, 191
  fundamentalist ideology 178–9,
    189–90
  growing influence 178–9
Guardian 160, 166
Gwynedd: large elderly population
  64

Hadrian's Wall 9
Halifax Building Society 190
Harding, Mike 155, 156
Harvey, Richard 97
Hastings, Sir Stephen 162
Heritage Coasts 104
Heritage industry 90–1, 100–1
Hertford, Marquis of 20, 25
Heseltine, Michael 124, 125, 140
Hewison, Robert: *The Heritage Industry*
  90–1
Highlands and Islands Development
  Board 131, 132
Holloway, John: 'The Myth of England'
  187
Home Counties 80
  artifically created shortage of building
    land 121
  rise in cost of building land 69
Hopkins, Gerard Manley: *Inversnaid* 89
Horse and Hound 161
House Builders Federation 124, 136
  on artificially created land shortage
    119–23 *passim*, 128
Housing in Britain
  artificially created land shortage
    119–25, 128, 182
  gap between design development and
    public perception 183–4
  houses built per annum, 1980s 123–4,
    184
  housing associations 125
  'isolated' housing in rural areas 184
  medieval 181
  need to release farmland for building
    125
  new housing required 123
  problem of cost of 'traditional'
    materials today 182
  subjectivity of design 182
  unfit for human habitation 124
Howitt, William: *The Rural Life of
  England* 147

ICI 39
Industrial Revolution 15, 16
Institute of Terrestrial Ecology 98

International Agricultural Trade Research
    Consortium 57

Jenkins, Simon 34
Jones Lang Wootton: *Decentralisation
    Report 1988* 80
Jopling, Michael 43

Labour Party 178
    commitment to abolish foxhunting
        160–1, 162
Lake District National Park 96, 103,
    109
    Lake Windermere 172
Less Favoured Areas 44, 51
Linseed 39
London
    commuters 78
    Docklands 80
    migration from 121
    salaries 80
London property boom, 1980s 69, 122
    incentive to move to country 62–3, 64,
        68–9
Lupins 39

McLaughlin, Brian: *Deprivation in Rural
    Areas* 70
Manpower Services Commission
    Community Programme 133
Meibion Glyndwr (Sons of Glendower)
    74
Merricks, Philip 55
Midlands: artificially created shortage of
    building land 120
Milton, John: *Paradise Lost* 147
Milton Keynes 137
Ministry of Agriculture 30, 31, 33, 36,
    37, 42, 45, 46, 53, 56, 107
    on effect of farming quotas 41, 42
Moorland Publishing 153
Moult, Ted 45

National Farmers Union 42, 44, 57, 108,
    136
National Heritage Memorial Fund 102,
    104

National Parks, British 21, 93–103,
    105–6, 128, 140, 156
    administration 96
    authorities' attitude to farming 101
    conservation v. tourism 98–9, 103
    criticisms of authorities running 95–6
    deleterious effects 22
    difference between British and US
        94–5
    establishment, 1950s 93
    government grants 96
    improving on nature 101
    justification for 102
    limitations on public access 102–3
    mostly privately owned 94, 95
    opposition to roads through 186–7
    underfinancing 99–100
    US concept 93
National Parks and Access to the
    Countryside Act, 1949 93, 107
National Trust 102, 104, 106, 136, 177
    allows foxhunting on land belonging to
        162
Nature Conservancy Council 50, 94, 102,
    104, 106
    pays farmer to set up Sheppey nature
        reserve 55
Needham, Tom 135, 136
Newby, Professor Howard 26
Nimby (Not In My Back Yard) syndrome
    129, 130, 139, 185
North of England
    artificially created shortage of building
        land 121–2
    conservation blight 109–10, 111, 117,
        186
    high unemployment 109, 110
    need for industrial development 109
    preponderant share of National Parks
        109
North Pennines Area of Outstanding
    Natural Beauty 107–9
    few jobs generated by 109
    grants 108
    High Force 155
    income from tourists 133
    Mickle Fell army training range 155

North Pennines Area *cont.*
  opposition to designation 108
  public inquiry into plan to designate
    108
  tourists 109
North-West England: artificially created
  shortage of building land 120
North York Moors National Park 95,
  186
  cost of destroying bracken, 1988 101
  Fylingdales early warning station 9,
    95
Northampton: relocation target for
  industry from London 185
Nuclear power 179

Oil-seed rape 39

Peak District National Park 96, 155
  'manages' sheep on East Moor
    102
Peel, Sir Robert 3
Pennine Way 155
Peterborough: relocation target for
  industry from London 185
Peterson, William 56
Pile, Stephen: on British dislike of cities
  127–8
Potatoes: as sources of starch 39

Ramblers Association 102, 186
  concern with public footpaths 154,
    157, 158, 164
  critical of farmers 156
  dislike of rural industries 156
  dissatisfaction with countryside
    authorities 156
  Forbidden Britain Day 155
  rambling 'philosophy' 154
  serves urbanite needs 153–4
Ridley, Nicholas 124, 130
  attempt to deal with planning
    restrictions 140–1
Rifkind, Malcolm 131
Rose, Simon 99
Royal Society for the Protection of Birds
  104, 106

Runcie, Dr Robert 73, 76
Ruralism
  boredom and loneliness among
    incomers 66
  commuting as disincentive to better
    services 72–3
  development of new squirearchy 70–1,
    85, 130
  division between incomers and locals
    67, 68
  drift from town to country 4, 61 *et seq.*
  easy accessibility of countryside 62
  expense of commuting 75
  incomers' opposition to factories and
    workshops 71
  magazines 'marketing' idea of 68
  make-up of migrants to country 64
  old people as strain on medical
    resources 72
  pretence in urbanized Britain re
    147–50
  problem of housing local people 69–70
    passim, 75
  reasons for younger people moving to
    country 64–5
  villagers' resistance to incomers 73–4

Sackville-West, Victoria: 'The Land' 3,
  5
Scotland
  artificially created shortage of building
    land 122
  conservation blight 117
  large elderly population in Borders 64
  no National Parks 22–3
  problem of Highlands' communications
    132
  'Silicon Valley' 132
  unemployment, 1987 131
Scottish Conservation Projects 159
Scottish Development Agency 131
Scottish Enterprise 131–2
Scottish National Party 22
Self-sufficiency
  'opting out of the rat-race' 62
  rural migrants 62, 65
Severely Disadvantaged Areas 51

Sheppey, Isle of: farm turned into nature
    reserve, 1987 55
Sherwood Forest: holidaymakers' village
    138
Shoard, Marion 155
    This Land is Our Land 48, 149, 150
Sites of Special Scientific Interest 55, 98,
    104, 107
Smaller Historic Towns and Villages
    Association, The 180–1
Smiles, Samuel 34
Snowdonia Park, 95
    Trawsfynydd nuclear power station 95
Somerset Levels 107
South Coast: large elderly population 64
South Downs 107
South-East England
    artificially created shortage of building
        land 121
    creeping suburbanization 186
    equal yearly exodus and intake of
        people 124, 140
    high population density 121
    land cost in price of new house 123
    low unemployment 110
    percentage of Green Belt or AONB
        area 129
    percentage of urban land 129
    property prices, 1980s 69
    question of rural development 139–40
    urban sprawl 117–18
South-West England
    artificially created shortage of building
        land 120–1
    cheaper housing than London's 63
    conservation blight 117
    influence of elderly on education and
        medicine 72
    influx from South-East England, 1986
        61
    large elderly population 63
    lower than average crime rate 63
    rise in cost of building land, 1980s 69
Southern Upland Way 159
Stukeley, William 15
Sunday Times: condemns farm lobby 34
Sunflowers 39

Sussex
    large elderly population 64
    property prices, 1980s 69
Swindon: relocation target for industry
    from London 185

Tenterden, Kent: condemnation of new
    leisure centre 181
Thatcher, Margaret 5, 34
Timber Growers UK 50
Tourism in Britain 133–4, 165–73
    annual earnings from 165, 169
    British ambivalence about 165–6, 170
    congestion caused by 135, 136
    disadvantages 134
    holiday homes and cottages 165–6,
        171–2, 173
    low status of service industries 168–9
    need for ministry of tourism 170
    need for regional tourism departments
        170
    need to exploit market in 169–73
    numbers employed in 165
    opposition to disruption of life by
        166
    problem of overcrowding 168
    time-sharing 172
    traffic problems 166–7
Town and country planning
    Act of 1947 126
    confines people in crowded areas 143
    incompatible with commercial growth
        in countryside 130
    public inquiry system 141–2
    See also Green Belts
Turner, Frederick J. 113–14

University Chest 55
US National Parks 93, 94

Villages
    controlling development of existing
        138–9
    creating new villages 137–8
    electronic cottages 139
    holidaymakers' 138, 172
    model village in Massachusetts 182–3

Wales
  anti-English arson and bombing
    campaign 74, 172
  arson in conifer plantations 189
  conservation blight 117
  resentment at English settlement 74
  rural enterprise policy 133
  tourism 133, 134
  'Watch over the National Parks' campaign
    104
Weather, 1980s: worldwide effect of
    warmth on crops 40
Welsh Office 133
West Indies: Bosques Colon
    tree-replacement project 112
Wight, Isle of: large elderly population 64
Wildlife Act 107
Wilson, Nicholas 125
Wisconsin University, US: man-made
    prairie 111–12

Woodforde, James 77
Worldwide ecological problems 178

Yellowstone National Park 93
Yorkshire Dales National Park 95, 96,
    109
  cost of damage by visitors, 1987 98
  damage done by walkers 98, 99, 103,
    152, 163
  management committee 96
  preservation of barns and walls 100
  repairs to paths 99
  tourists 97
  Visitor newsletter 99
Yorkshire, North
  artificially created shortage of building
    land 122
  cost of Dales cottages, 1989 78–9,
    122
  large elderly population 64